THE COMMON MARKET

Robert Gurland and Anthony MacLean

THE COMMON MARKET

A Commonsense guide for Americans

**PADDINGTON
PRESS LTD**

**THE TWO CONTINENTS
PUBLISHING GROUP**

NOTICE

The details of tax and other regulations cited in this book were accurate at the time they were printed. The laws of all lands are in a constant state of change. This is particularly true of the EEC countries which adapt their laws to meet Common Market requirements. Therefore those details should be read as a guide to further inquiry rather than a rule of what exists today.

Library of Congress Cataloging in Publication Data

Gurland, Robert.
    The Common Market.

    1. European Economic Community. 2. European Eco-
nomic Community--United States. I. MacLean, Anthony,
joint author. II. Title.
HC241.2.G87   338'.9142   73-15028
ISBN 0-8467-0024-7

© Copyright Paddington Press Ltd 1974
Printed in the U.S.A.
Designed by Richard Johnson
Illustrations by the Diagram Group,
London, England
ISBN 0–8467–0024–7
Library of Congress Catalog Card No. 73–15028

IN THE U.S.A.
PADDINGTON PRESS LTD
TWO CONTINENTS
PUBLISHING GROUP
30 East 42nd Street
New York City, New York 10017

IN THE UNITED KINGDOM
PADDINGTON PRESS LTD
1 Wardour Street
London W1

IN CANADA
PADDINGTON PRESS LTD
distributed by
RANDOM HOUSE OF CANADA
370 Alliance Avenue
Toronto, Ontario   76-3107

CONTENTS

AUTHOR'S NOTE

I would like to acknowledge the contributions and assistance rendered to me by many colleagues throughout the EEC and in the U.S.A. Their generous and professional comments were always given constructively and with care and concern.

My particular appreciation goes to Joel Kaye, an English barrister, and Arthur Gellman, an American lawyer, associates in my office who did much of the basic research and to Richard Zeif of the New York Bar for his encouragement and advice.

Finally I dedicate this book to my parents, Dr and Mrs Irving Gurland, and my good friend Dick Forhan. Their memory is with me.
Robert Gurland
London, England
1974

Robert Gurland was born in New York, on August 8, 1931. He is a member of the Bar of the state of New York and is admitted to practice before the U.S. Supreme Court and the U.S. Tax Court: Author of "Taxation Without Representation" published in 1973 in London: Contributing Editor of The International Tax Report, tax columnist for Overseas Newsletter for Americans: Senior partner in the International Law firm of Buechner, Gurland & Partners with offices in London, Brussels and Munich.

PREFACE

On January 1, 1973, with the addition of the United Kingdom, the Irish Republic, and Denmark to the original six Members, the European Economic Community (known colloquially as the Common Market) joined the ranks of one of the world's largest commercial trading areas. It is evident that the Common Market will develop into an even more powerful economic force. The international energy crisis has only underlined the fact that it is no longer possible for each Common Market country to form its policy independent of its neighbors. It is increasingly apparent that the American and Canadian businessman must understand the Europeans, their policies, and commercial attitudes if he wishes to be successful. For the enterprising, an extensive familiarity with the Common Market, its structure and the nature of its operations is essential.

Europe has arisen 'Pheonix-like' from the ruins of World War II. Eurocrats (officials of the EEC) in Brussels and Strassburg exercise as much influence over the continent's future as do the individual parliaments of the constituent member nations of the Common Market.

Organized in 1957 the EEC has already grown into a strong economic and political unit. The future trading and political potential of the Common Market is even more vast. It has become clear that the exchange rates of the dollar, the yen and other currencies are inextricably linked with the monetary policy of the EEC.

In the flood of publications which have accompanied the development of the Common Market, little has been done to help the enterprising (non-European) businessman wishing to take full advantage of the opportunites now open to him in Western Europe.

Businessmen within each country are necessarily familiar with the territory in which they operate. They know the outline of their country's financial regulations, commercial rules and tax laws as they relate to their businesses. They know what professional services are available to them. If they do not know all the answers to their problems, they know what these problems are and they know where to find some of the answers.

This book hopes to aid the American entrepreneur by providing a guide to commercial activities in the Common Market. It describes local situations and provides a brief profile for each country in the EEC. Also included are references to most of the important regulations with which businessmen should be familiar. Finally there are forecasts of the ways in which the European Economic Community is likely to develop over the next few years. The areas which the enterprising businessman may find commercially attractive or potentially troublesome are also highlighted.

It is intended to give both the American and European points of view to help one become aware of the dangers, the problems, the opportunities and the facts of international economic life. The United States and its businessmen must learn to cope, live, and work with the Common Market (as well as other international market forces).

Above all, this book intends to be informative and of interest to everyone concerned about the world in which we live. While it should be of interest to all, the book is directed primarily toward Americans, as The United States is the largest single investor nation in the Common Market. While United States policy has generally favored the Common Market and supported European industrial progress, U.S. short and medium term interests are not always the same as those of Europe. Conflict between the U.S.A. and the Common Market is with us; the outcome of this conflict will be a crucial factor in determining the future quality of life on both sides of the Atlantic.

Perhaps the need for this book is best expressed in the results of a recent Gallup poll about the Common Market, which indicated that most Americans have never heard of the Common Market—in spite of the fact that the EEC is the second largest trading partner (after Canada) of the United States. More significantly, most American businessmen are not even familiar with the rudimentary aspects of the history, structure, operation, impact and effect of the Common Market. It is not only important for non-Europeans to know about the Common Market—it is important to understand what the Common Market thinks of Americans and how it intends to deal with them. In this way those Americans who live, travel, work, manufacture, buy, sell, and invest abroad can learn how to deal effectively, profitably, and constructively with it.

Americans have come to realize that there are profoundly complicated challenges inherent in their influence and power. America's ability to maintain a viable, economic 'presence' in Europe has turned out to be far more important than the maintenance of an American military 'presence' in Europe. While most European countries desire foreign capital and technology they are also fearful of the power and potentially disruptive influence of that foreign economic 'presence'. Many European policy makers are well aware that there are a

number of American companies so large that their annual gross
product is more than the gross national product (GNP) of nations the
size of Ireland. They are aware of the dramatic fact that a company such
as General Motors has more net worth than all of the non-American
stock exchanges of the world except for the London Stock Exchange.
This consciousness and concern on the part of the Common Market in
preventing 'foreigners' from 'taking over' is primarily based on the huge
economic power of a relatively small number of American
'multi-national' companies. The attitudes arising out of the continuing
debates on how to effectively control the giant 'multi-nationals'
permeates to some degree Common Market policy and actions with
respect to much smaller 'foreign' businesses.

Europeans within the Common Market are also very conscious of the
role played by the Eurodollar (excess U.S. cash held by American
businesses in Europe) in the periodic monetary crises that have taken
place throughout the current history of the Common Market. Eurodollars and Eurobonds originated as a result of the accumulation of
excess U.S. dollars by American companies doing business outside the
U.S.A. It seemed a good idea to use these surpluses to finance
overseas operations. Luxembourg and London became the main
centers for these offerings. The dimensions of the Eurodollar presence
within the Common Market is so significant that Common Market
monetary officials are constantly compelled to consider this factor in the
development of fiscal policy. France has periodically sought Common
Market agreement for strong curbs on the estimated one hundred
billion Eurodollars which 'clutters' the international money market.
This situation however is not static and recently American domination
of the Eurodollar and Eurobond market has been changing. Stable
European currencies within the Common Market have made their own
impact on this market.

The Europeans want to stand on their own feet. They
understandably do not want their labor to be employed for foreign
development and their economy controlled and exploited by strangers.
The EEC wants to develop a European identity and be independent of
the super-powers.

In April 1945 the war in Europe came to an end. Western Europe
had been devastated, occupied, blitzed and bankrupted. Its people had
been slaughtered and enervated. The United States of America was then
the greatest military and economic power in the world. Europe looked
to the States for the support and assistance in peace time which it had
so effectively provided during the War. At that time no European
currency was stable and its value was subject to constant questioning.
The dollar together with American cigarettes, chewing gum,
chocolate bars and nylon stockings was in many respects the best

9

currency in Europe.

In 1957 the American economy was booming. The growth and expansion of American policies and ideals was a matter of international political fact. World politics was largely the story of the relationship between the two super-powers—the U.S.A. and the Soviet Union. It was not surprising that the countries of western Europe, especially Britain and Germany, looked to a vigorous, wealthy and powerful United States of America for leadership in foreign and domestic policy. American business was flourishing in Europe. The dollar enjoyed a favorable exchange rate against all European currencies. In practical terms, the world was on the dollar standard—not the gold standard. American voices could be heard in most of the business establishments around Europe.

United States aid to Europe after World War II, under the Marshall plan, was about twelve billion dollars. On recent values that would be at least twenty billion dollars. By 1973, on the other hand, the United States had short term debts to Europe of about eighty billion dollars. This is an extraordinary reversal and was primarily due to the poor balance of payments situation in the U.S.A. that had prevailed for many years.

By 1973 U.S. foreign direct investment abroad had reached one hundred billion dollars. Between 1960 and 1973 foreign investment in the U.S.A. more than doubled from under seven billion dollars to over fifteen billion dollars. Of this sum almost one half came from two Common Market countries (over four billion dollars from Great Britain and more than two billion from the Netherlands).

Merryll, Lynch, Pearce, Fenner and Smith, the largest United States stockbrokers in the world, did over one billion dollars of international financing in 1972 alone. Improvement in the United States balance of payments in the year 1973 was due in many respects to the long term investment policy in the U.S.A. by foreigners. About one and one third billion dollars came into the States in the third quarter of that year. During the same period American foreign investment fell by seven hundred million dollars.

American companies earn about two and a half billion dollars each year from their European investments whereas the reverse flow is a very small fraction of that amount.

In spite of the radical changes that have taken place in the relative positions of the United States and the Common Market countries, Europe's trading and defense requirements still serve to bind it to the U.S.A. It is apparent to all that Europe needs today, and in the future, a strong ploitical and economic relationship with America, and America needs Europe.

Aside from historical, commercial and country to country

relationships as well as ethnic links, the United States is bound to
Western Europe as a whole by the following Institutions:

1. The International Monetary Fund (IMF) and the World Bank
were both established at Bretton Woods in 1946. The U.S.A.
contributes approximately 28% of the IMF and Europe contributes
approximately 16%.

2. General Agreement in Tariffs and Trade (GATT), while never
formally ratified by any country, over one hundred nations adhere
to its rules to promote free trade.

3. The United Nations and its agencies were created at the end of
World War II. Many of its agencies and the United Nations itself
often address themselves to a broad range of economic questions
involving Western Europe and the U.S.A.

4. The North Atlantic Treaty Organization (NATO) was created in
1949 and includes all Western European countries, except Sweden and
Switzerland.

The EEC was born when the six founding countries signed the
EEC Treaty of Rome in March, 1957. As far as America is
concerned it was the birth of the most significant trading block in the
world. The EEC quickly became known as the 'Common Market'—it is
in fact a very un-common market and represents one of the most
significant social, political and economic developments in modern
times. Today nine countries make up the Common Market.

Consider the improbability of it all. Nine countries with seven
major, and at least four minor languages; with varying social, legal and
political structures, all founded on systems evolved over many
centuries, put aside their vast differences and prejudices, and by
agreement made a common front to compete in today's world.

Today these Common Market countries confront together the
problems of complex technology, inflation, energy, booming population
and enormous social pressures. The days of the rugged individualist
and pioneer nations are gone. This is an era of size, specialization,
technology, emerging nations, and finance.

From the European's point of view, World War II destroyed an
age-old idea that the State was all powerful and capable of protecting its
citizens. They now recognize that inter-dependence is the key to
modern political thought and economic survival—not independence.

The European Coal and Steel Community, the forerunner of the EEC,
was primarily based on the concept that by removing the essential
resources from national control, two traditional enemies, France and
Germany, would remain at peace. So far it has worked. The production
of guns, tanks and other weapons is now under the 'extra-national'
control of the EEC. Europe has already reaped considerable economic
benefits from that concept, including the reduction of excess and

11

overlapping facilities and the creation of a larger 'Common Market' for coal and steel.

The United States and all of its businessmen are now faced with the reality of the Common Market and the necessity of having to work in harmony with it. As the most 'multi-national' nation in the world this job should be effectively accomplished—provided that the U.S.A. draws upon her reserves of talent, technology, energy, thoughtfulness, and ethnic mix which are all part of her true 'natural resources'.

The purpose of this book is to provide a practical understanding of how to conduct oneself commercially with this new 'United States of Europe'.

I History of the Common Market

The European Economic Community is still in its infancy. So far its record according to some few cynics has not been very impressive. It has in fact not yet achieved many of the aims of its creators. It is not quite the kind of world force some foresaw. Its detractors say it will not survive. But give it time. The genie is out of the bottle and today the EEC is very much a force to be considered by non-Europeans in any relationship or transaction with any European country.

When the original six founding countries signed the EEC Treaty of Rome in March, 1957, it was an event which may yet prove to be as important and impressive as the signing of the Declaration of Independence. Indeed the EEC is often called "The United States of Europe."

How did it all begin?

In 1948 the Benelux countries (Belgium, Holland and Luxembourg) formed a free trade area, or "customs union", under the GATT (General Agreement on Trade and Tariffs) principles. These principles provide in part that neighboring countries should combine to eliminate their common border taxes while establishing a common import duty frontier with respect to the rest of the world. One benefit is that small nations can reduce the price of their export goods by lowering the cost of input-imports and raw materials acquired from their partner-neighbors. This promotes world trade and aids their balance of payments.

The Benelux countries, together with France, Germany and Italy, formed the European Coal and Steel Community in 1951. As its name implies this agreement served to combine the effective use of the coal and steel resources of those countries. The Commission of the Coal and Steel Community had the power to fix prices for those commodities. However, the European Coal and Steel Community (ECSC) was more than a pooling of assets. It established the principle that industrial and technological changes should not come about at the expense of labor. For the first time, workers in those countries are being retrained and resettled, while being paid, after jobs are lost.

In Rome in 1957 the European Atomic Energy Commission
(EURATOM) was organized by the same six nations—for obvious
reasons.

On the same day (March 25, 1957) another Treaty of Rome was
signed organizing the EEC commencing January 1, 1958. (All
references to "The Treaty of Rome" will be to the EEC treaty.) Its
principal aim was to improve the living and working conditions of the
people in the EEC by establishing a common trade area or "Common
Market".

So it was that twelve years after the end of World War II, Europe
felt strong enough to stand on its new feet—having learned from hard
experience that it could not survive in the old tradition.

While all this was going on other European countries were not
standing idly by. Great Britain refused in 1950 to join the ECSC. For
ten years France, under De Gaulle, opposed Britain's entry into the
Common Market. Great Britain, together with Denmark, Norway,
Austria, Portugal, Sweden and Switzerland (with Finland as an
associate member) formed the EFTA (European Free Trade
Association) to counterbalance the effects of the EEC.

In 1972 Great Britain, Ireland and Denmark were admitted to the
EEC, effective January 1, 1973. Special trade agreements were made
between the EEC and the remaining EFTA countries.

The European Monetary Fund (EMF) was established under EEC
auspices in Luxembourg in April, 1973. It was intended to be the
nucleus of a Common Market central banking system. By 1980 it was
hoped that all of the gold reserves of the EEC countries would be
pooled in the EMF. ($44 billion in 1972, about four times that of the
U.S.A.)

All of these associations and agreements required the participating
countries to surrender some of their independence to the central
authority of the new group. Such steps are not taken lightly; neither
are they accepted freely. It was one thing for thirteen new colonies in
America to form a new nation in a new world. It is a far more
difficult task for nine old, proud colonizers to accept the reality of their
decline from independent power and to admit to others (some of whom
have been their enemies for centuries) that they could not stand alone.

The American Parallel

America was born oceans apart from the rest of the world and
remained substantially separated by lack of communications for
almost two centuries. The Common Market was born in the midst of
the technological revolution where obstacles to communication are
broken every day. The Civil War in the U.S.A. cost more lives than any
other American war and the wounds it caused have not yet fully healed. 15

It was fought over the question of "states rights"—over the issue of whether the individual state governments or the Federal government had the right to determine questions of national policy and taxation.

The Common Market has yet to fully resolve its "states rights" questions. The French seem to lean towards the confederacy concept while the Benelux countries and Germany stand more for the union. But there is no doubt that the structure of the EEC is federal in concept rather than merely associative; and must become more so in the course of time. One of the effects of the Arab oil crisis in 1973 was a call by the leaders of Germany, France and England for the development of a "European" foreign policy.

These concepts of true federation are not easily accepted. Europe has its "states righters." Some of these battles are still to be fought. But the "negative" positions of people like De Gaulle and Pompidou of France and Enoch Powell and Harold Wilson of England will have little impact on the long term future of the Common Market. Its birth, growth and concepts will influence us all.

International aspects of the EEC

It would be foolish to say that the creation of the EEC is a local situation, the effects of which are only to be felt in Europe. Almost from the start the European Community became an international community. In 1964 under the Yaounde convention, the following nineteen countries became associates of the EEC—they had been colonies of EEC members:

Mauritania, Mali, Senegal, Ivory Coast, Upper Volta,
Niger Togo, Dahomey, Cameroon, Chad, Centrafrican Republic,
Gabon, Congo, Zaire, Rwanda, Burundi, Madagascar,
Mauritius and Somalia.

Most of these nations are French-speaking and former colonies of France and Belgium.

Under the Arusha convention of 1968 Kenya, Uganda and Tanzania became associates of the EEC. In the following year Morocco and Tunisia joined as associates. Since 1958 the following countries were the first to develop special relationships with the EEC effectively reducing trade barriers between themselves and the Common Market:

Greece, Turkey, Spain, Malta and Yugoslavia.

In 1972, as part of the package for admission of the United Kingdom, Denmark and Eire, the Common Market agreed to have special relationships with the other EFTA countries—Austria, Portugal, Sweden, Switzerland and Norway. Similar free trade arrangements have been made with Finland which was an EFTA associate.

The EEC now has nine members with a population of over 250 million and thirty-five European, Scandinavian and African

16

associates. This is clearly a world economic force to be reckoned with!

The international financial impact of the Common Market

Since the EEC has concluded agreements with all of the EFTA countries and Finland, no new trade barriers will be erected in Western Europe or Scandinavia. There are some minor exceptions to this rule. Certain goods are considered sensitive (such as paper, cork, textiles and some aluminium metal products). These will be subject to quotas, and these tariffs will not be abolished until 1985. Also, stricter rules regarding the country of origin of the goods will apply between EFTA and EEC countries than apply between the EEC countries themselves.

With these few exceptions, when the last tariffs between the EEC and EFTA are abolished on July 1, 1977, it will coincide with the abolition of tariffs between all EEC countries. At that time there will be a European duty-free market for about 400 million people in eighteen industrialized countries with a geographical area of over 1,500,000 square miles (U.S.—3,600,000 square miles); a GNP (gross national product) for the EEC for the Year 1972 of about $781 billion (approximately 65% of the U.S.A.); and gold reserves for the EEC for the year 1972 of $44 billion (U.S. about $11 billion).

The Common Market is also negotiating trade agreements with many other countries, including some in the Caribbean and the Pacific.

In Latin America agreement has been reached with Brazil, Uraguay and Argentina; and, in the Middle East, with Iran.

Perhaps the most important of all these agreements is the Commercial Cooperation Agreement of December, 1973, between the EEC and India. This is the first treaty of its kind. It establishes the two areas as political equals, a status much sought by India. In addition to the usual trade concessions, the treaty establishes the procedures for developing future economic cooperation. A mixed committe of Indian representatives and members of both the EEC Council and Commission will work out the new economic relationships. This agreement clearly identifies the EEC as an independent political unit and might well be a standard for future agreements.

The American Connection and Presence

In 1971 the EEC accounted for one-fifth of all world trade not including trade between the nine EEC countries temselves. Only the U.S.A. exceeded them.

The purchasing power of those countries has been almost twice that of the U.S. between 1958 and 1971. That's food for thought.

On December 14, 1973, the Common Market Nine issued their first united policy document since the Treaty of Rome. That document calls

17

for a common defense policy and the right to be treated as equals by the U.S.A. They confirmed their belief in a united Europe under the Treaty of Rome and pledged to increase their efforts towards harmonization of their affairs.

However, Americans should be aware that American-owned production in Europe represents Europe's single largest industrial power. This means that the Common Market must in all of its policies and actions consider the economic power of the United States of America within the Common Market itself. This presents new opportunities but also creates new tensions and areas of concern.

The following are just a very *few* examples of the type of American "multinational" presence which the UN and EEC are concerned about.

1. As a result of negotiations between the U.S. Atomic Energy Commission (A.E.C.) and Euratom, the European Commission has agreed to purchase approximately 120 tons of uranium at a cost of $9 million. The uranium will be enriched in the U.S.A. and transferred to the A.E.C., which in turn will lease it to Euratom for research in Europe. They will have an option to buy the materials at 1973 prices over the next few years. So uranium rich America has a hold on uranium poor Europe and the Europeans resent the A.E.C. "forcing" them to make long term commitments for enriched uranium.

Due to a lack of cooperation in Euratom, two nuclear industries have developed in Europe. France has her system EURODIF—France, Belgium, Italy and Spain. It is expensive; but ready to go. Britain, Germany and Holland have another URENCO. It is more advanced; but far from completion. Consequently, the U.S. will probably be able to sell nuclear power stations and facilities to Europe for a long time in the future during the continuing energy crisis. This will have a dramatic effect on the balance of payments as the energy crisis makes the need for nuclear power all the greater.

The goal of both European groups is to become self-sufficient in nuclear technology and enriched uranium by 1980. Yet, ENEL, Italy's electricity company has recently ordered two more nuclear power plants from U.S. companies. This will make a total, in Italy, of six plants, five of which are American made (G.E. and Westinghouse). France itself, the most anti-American country in the EEC, has ordered two more nuclear plants which will use U.S. General Electric systems.

2. IBM controls 60% of the EEC computer market and grows 20% a year within that market. An additional 30% of this market is based on American technology.

The EEC Commission is determined to break this stranglehold and wants the EEC computer industry to be regrouped to become competitive with IBM. This would require ICL of Great Britain to merge with UNIDATA [which combines Philips (Holland), Siemens

18

(Germany), and CII (France)]. It will not come about for some time as ICL wants to "go it alone" for the time being.

3. U.S. based contractors obtained almost two-thirds of all orders placed in Western Europe for the construction of petroleum and chemical plants in the year from June 1972 to June 1973. This is a continuation of the domination of the United States companies in this field since World War II—and it is increasing. Western Europe is the most important market for export contracting services according to a survey by the trade journal *Chemical Age International.*

An analysis of the chemical industry shows that the turnover of all U.S. companies for 1971 was $50 billion as compared to the turnover for all the EEC's chemical companies of $45 billion. However, the Common Market companies earn more of their income abroad than do U.S. companies.

In 1973, the three largest investors in the West German chemical industry were Texaco, Dow Chemical and Mobil Oil. Dupont will shortly build a $100 million plant in the Sterling Area (Britain or Ireland) to produce titanium dioxide.

4. Within the five year period from 1968 to 1973, 108 U.S. bank offices were opened within the Common Market. Of these, forty are in Britain with nineteen each in Germany and France.

5. Among the biggest selling cars in Europe are England's Ford and Germany's Opel (General Motors).

6. Nearly one-third of Owens Illinois' (the world's largest glass manufacturer) profits come from non-U.S. sources. It owns interests in the two largest European glass container manufacturers, United Glass in England (50%) and Garresheim in Germany (76%). It also owns two corrugated case factories (it is the largest U.S. producer of corrugated cases).

As is the case with most multi-nationals, their international division is based in their home office, Toledo, Ohio. Subsidiaries are required to report and account to the home office rather than to a European headquarters.

7. A report issued in September, 1973, by the Electronic Commission of the *French Five Year Social and Economic Development Plan* stated that over 60% of French production of electronic, data processing and telecommunication equipment is controlled by subsidiaries of foreign firms—mainly American; and foreign penetration is increasing.

8. U.S. investment in Ireland has created about 25% (or 16,000) of the new jobs in Ireland since 1960. There are approximately 130 U.S. companies in Ireland with assets of about $212 million.

9. (A) It is estimated that there are over 80 U.S. companies in Wales (Great Britain) employing over 40,000 people with a payroll in excess of

19

$125 million per year. The investment of these companies exceeds $750 million.

(B) The schedule of the 75 largest U.K. exporters for 1972 shows that many are foreign (non-British) companies—most of which are American.

(C) The U.S.A. Carborundum company owns the famous British Chinaware company Spode. Approximately 40% of Carborundum's sales come from its overseas operation—(about $150 million).

The EEC and GATT and the 3rd World

The General Agreement on Trade and Tariffs (GATT) was organized in Havana in 1947. Although it has no statutory authority (since only one country has ratified it), it exerts a great influence on world trade. Its aim is to reduce trade barriers between nations.

Under the GATT system, any proposed customs union must be able to demonstrate that it is a single unit for trade purposes. This is forcing the nine EEC countries to change their internal border tax regulations to maintain their GATT status. At present, there exists a complex system of border taxes which delays shipments, affects prices and is destructive to EEC policy. In time they must be uniform. A new system of customs forms in the EEC will shortly replace the existing multi-form methods with one "all purpose" form known as EUR 1.

Developing countries form two-thirds of GATT members, 102 attended the Tokyo conference of GATT in 1973.

The "Third World" is an unofficial designation for all of the "emerging" nations of the world. Underdeveloped and "backward" by Western standards they represent much of the population and resources of the world. Their power and influence is growing daily. The U.S.A., Russia, China, and the EEC are battling for influence in the Third World.

The EEC is negotiating with 42 African countries regarding the development of a "special relationship" with them. As most of those countries are former colonies of Britain and France, the basis for such an arrangement exists in history and personal and corporate relationships.

The major contention between the West and the Third World in GATT negotiations relates to reciprocal customs taxes. The poorer nations do not want reciprocity to act to their detriment. They want to be able to tax their imports from rich nations which in turn should permit imports of goods from Third World countries at low rates of tax. This they feel would be fairer than equal rates of tax as it improves the ability of poor countries to compete with the highly developed nations.

Latin American countries are concerned mainly with the sale of beef to the EEC at the best prices. Since beef is in short supply they hope to negotiate advantageous concessions from the EEC.

After the 1973 war between the Arab states and Israel, most of the major Arab oil producing countries reduced, and in some cases cut off oil shipments to their large customers. This caused world chaos and dissension within the Common Market itself. It also created a new global influence. Oil is being used in a sophisticated way as a political weapon. During that crisis its EEC/NATO allies did not support the U.S.A. The primary reason—oil. EEC policy will increasingly be influenced by the Third World. Oil producing countries have gained enormous financial reserves which are being used in much the same way the U.S.A. and the USSR use their wealth and power—to make friends and influence people.

The Arab nations have 8% of the vote in the IMF (International Monetary Fund) and their surpluses with the IMF in 1973 were about $15 billion. Within ten years these surpluses are estimated to reach $50 billion. With increased revenues from higher oil prices their share of world income will increase. They will demand more of a voice in the IMF and in all other international agencies and arrangements. The wealthy oil producing countries often prefer Europe for their "home away from home", business, education and socializing.

The International Monetary Fund predicted in 1972 that the United States will have a trade surplus of $4 billion in 1974 and the Arab oil producers will have twice that much—$8 billion. That was before the sharp rise in the price of oil. Europe, Japan and the developing nations will have to pay the bills. There will be deficits in the balance of payments of many EEC countries. On balance the EEC hopes to break even. The danger of economic dissension on this issue is severe.

The U.S. wants to deal with NATO, GATT, monetary reform and its EEC relationship as a whole rather than as separate issues. This the EEC will not do.

Under GATT rules, the U.S. has claims against the Common Market which are more than ten years old and relate to improper imposition of tariffs by the EEC against U.S. agricultural products. The entry of Britain, Ireland and Denmark into the Community adds greatly to such claims and it is an issue that has generated considerable resentment and anger in many U.S. political and economic policy centers.

The EEC on the other hand is angry about U.S. tax laws creating DISCs (Domestic International Sales Companies) which they feel give U.S. companies a tax advantage in the export field. DISCs can defer 50% of their tax if their income is from the sale of U.S. products outside the U.S.A. Whether or not this violates GATT rules is yet to be decided. Since DISCs are relatively new their true impact on foreign trade will not be known for some time but the Common Market views 21 this U.S. tax vehicle as contrary to their interests and to a previously accepted general understanding.

Through all of the short history of the Common Market with all of its unresolved questions its growing power and unity has to be regarded as a modern miracle. Its growth and development may be uneven and crisis and conflict ridden but it has matured and solidified year by year. It is now a reality and a functioning international force.

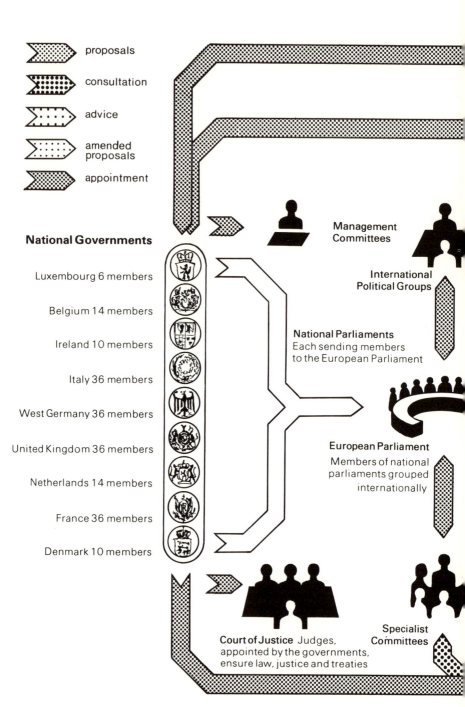

proposals

consultation

advice

amended proposals

appointment

National Governments

Luxembourg 6 members

Belgium 14 members

Ireland 10 members

Italy 36 members

West Germany 36 members

United Kingdom 36 members

Netherlands 14 members

France 36 members

Denmark 10 members

Management Committees

International Political Groups

National Parliaments
Each sending members to the European Parliament

European Parliament
Members of national parliaments grouped internationally

Specialist Committees

Court of Justice Judges, appointed by the governments, ensure law, justice and treaties

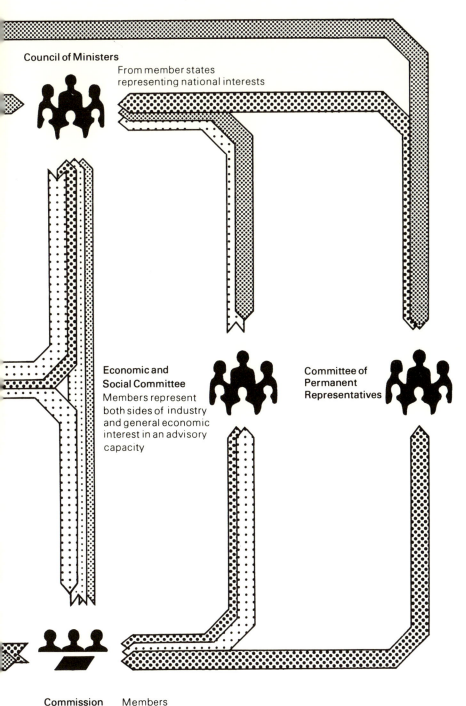

Council of Ministers From member states
representing national interests

**Economic and
Social Committee**
Members represent
both sides of industry
and general economic
interest in an advisory
capacity

**Committee of
Permanent
Representatives**

Commission Members
appointed by governments
but act independently

II How the Common Market operates

The political organization of the EEC is made up essentially of the Assembly; the Council of Ministers; the Commission; the Court of Justice; and Committees. An administrative apparatus of approximately eight thousand employees support and administer the structure.

The *Assembly* is roughly equivalent to the U.S. House of Representatives or the English Parliament. In fact it is commonly called the European Parliament. It is composed of members chosen according to the size of the member states they represent. The European Parliament has 198 representatives. France, Germany, Italy and the United Kingdom each have 36, while Belgium and the Netherlands are allowed 14, with ten for both Ireland and Denmark. Luxembourg has six.

It has little specific and overt power; but exercises a degree of political control and influence and is a deliberative and coordinating body. As Europe develops into a more cohesive political unit, the power of the European Parliament will increase.

The Council of Ministers might be loosely compared to the U.S. Senate although it does have some executive powers in addition to its legislative role. It makes most of the important decisions for the Community and is responsible for carrying out the objectives of the Treaty of Rome.

The Council has 9 members. Each state sends one representative; usually its foreign minister; but they have unequal power when voting on a proposal of the EEC Commission requiring a "qualified majority". The representatives of the four largest countries, in such cases, have 10 votes each. Holland and Belgium five votes each, whereas Ireland and Denmark are allowed three and little Luxembourg has two—for a total of 58. Usually 41 votes are required to pass proposals. Where the vote is on a matter not sponsored by the Commission the majority of 41 must come from six or more countries. The Presidency of the Council rotates every six months. The Council is assisted in its work by the *Committee of Permanent Representatives* consisting of a permanent representative from each state.

The Commission—consists of 13 full time members, no more than two of which can come from any one member state (two each from Great Britain, France, Germany, and Italy and one from each of the other countries). The Commission initiates, prepares and recommends proposals to the Council and gives opinions on EEC matters. It also participates in the work of the Assembly and the Council. It has executive power to carry out the instructions of the Council.

Commission members are appointed by agreement between the nine governments. *Members are obliged to act independently of their government's orders.* This has already caused some commission members problems in countries where there have been disputes over conflicting national and European interests. The Commission can be disciplined only by the Parliament (The Assembly) which can compel the entire Commission to resign.

The Court of Justice is crudely comparable to The United States Supreme Court. It consists of nine Judges appointed for six years by mutual consent of the member governments and three Advocates-General to assist the Court. All are allegedly chosen for their ability rather than their nationality. The Court is confined to the interpretation and administration of Community Law and is not a substitute for the courts of member states. It does not have full judicial powers but attempts to guard the supremacy of Community Law over national laws where there may be conflict.

General Organization

A treaty was signed in May, 1965, taking effect on July 1, 1969, merging the Councils of the European Coal and Steel Community, Euratom and the EEC into one Council. When voting on ECSC matters a simple majority vote is usually sufficient. It also merged the Commissions of the EEC and Euratom with the "High Authority" of the European Coal and Steel Community into a single Commission.

The Council and Commission are assisted by the Economic and Social Committee (144 members) for EEC and Euratom matters, and the Consultative Committee (81 members) for coal and steel matters. These committees consist of representatives from various levels of economic and social life throughout the market such as workers (one-third), employers (one-third) and farmers, unions and trade associations (one-third).

The Council issues Regulations (binding); Directives (binding as to ends; but not as to means): Decisions (binding); and Recommendations and Opinions (not binding).

The Commission issues Decisions (which are binding); Recommendations (binding as to ends; but not as to means); and Opinions (not binding) to carry out the principles of the Treaty of Rome and the instructions of the Council.

27

None of these institutions could have any power unless the member states in creating them, had given up a degree of their corresponding sovereignty in those areas. Therefore, it can be said that the EEC is more than a treaty or contract between nations. It is also an interlocking chain of obligations between those nations and the EEC itself. The result is a new international—or supernational entity—or federation; the EEC having the Treaty of Rome as its Constitution. European Community Law can therefore be somewhat likened to U.S. Federal Law. The power comes from the States; but in the end this grant of powers creates a federal body in some respects more powerful than the States themselves.

The authority to enter into agreements on behalf of the EEC with non-member nations rests with the Council, although the Commission is usually the instigator and the negotiator of such agreements.

Such authority has resulted in the several trade agreements between the EEC and nations outside the Community. In the future it is expected that this power will be extended into other areas such as monetary reform and international diplomatic relations.

The EEC program for future integration is headed by several major monetary measures leading ultimately to full financial integration. Regional development, an energy program, social welfare and harmonization of tax and business laws will also be forthcoming.

Consequently, the Community, its institutions and activities are to be regarded in much the same way as any formally created nation is regarded in its relations with other nations.

It can be expected to see "Community Law" gradually becoming in many areas the Law of the nine member nations to avoid confusion and to harmonize their inter-relationships.

Additionally there is a strong feeling for giving more power to the Commission and the Parliament and thereby limiting the influence of the Council.

It is interesting to note that in light of the criticism often levelled at the bureaucratic structure of the EEC its total number of employees as of the middle of 1974 was somewhat less than 8,000. The majority of these personnel are located in Brussels with the remainder spread throughout EEC offices elsewhere. This is a dramatically low figure when one considers that the British Department of Agriculture alone, in a country that is not primarily agricultural, has more than 8,000 employees in that one Governmental ministry.

Law

The original six Common Market nations agreed to give "full faith and credit" to each other's civil and commercial court rulings. Soon the other three will join them in ratifying this convention. Its interpretation is left to the European Court of Justice in Luxembourg. This is a major step towards the establishment of a federal Europe.

A particular problem for the new members and the U.S.A. is the fact that most members of the EEC are governed by Civil Law rather than Common Law. (Denmark has a legal system which is altogether different from any of these).

The essential differences between the Civil Law and Common Law systems is that Civil Law consists mainly of statutes or codes in which the laws and the principles on which they are based are fully set forth so the judges' rulings are deductive rather than inductive. Judges in Civil Law countries are specially trained and are aloof from the bar. Their decisions and courtroom work are more anonymous and written than are the personalized, oral labors of judges and lawyers in Common Law countries such as the United Kingdom, Ireland and the U.S.A. Under the Common Law every case makes its own law and precedents are most important. Statutes may be quite detailed; but their specific applied meaning is often omitted from legislation. The judge, therefore, becomes a "legislator" when he interprets the meaning of the statute or case (inductive reasoning). Judges in Common Law countries are trained as lawyers before they become judges.

While English is the most widely understood language in the Common Market, there is no doubt that French is presently the primary language of the EEC. It is the common language required to be used by all Common Market judges—regardless of their nationality— in their deliberations. In the treaties (which are written in several languages—each text being equal to the others) French legal concepts seem to predominate.

Unlike most American judges, EEC jurists often go far outside the wording of a given piece of legislation in order to determine its meaning and the intention of the legislators. This again highlights the differences between the Civil Law and Common Law systems. Strangely enough, although France is a Civil Law nation (the Code Napoleon), and in spite of French influence on EEC law, Common Law concepts still (the case law system) seem to be the basis for much of the Court of Justice's judicial deliberations. This does not occur by the usual system of precedents, which is prohibited in Civil Law systems; (every case must be judged on its own merits); but rather by "interpretation" of the law. Normally, Civil Law courts and judges do not have the power to "interpret" law and precedents do not count for very much. Yet in the EEC, the Common Market courts often exert a legislative function. This tendency is most evidenced in the administrative courts dealing with claims involving EEC agencies where the scope for relying upon precedents is greatest.

As is the case in France the Common Market Court of Justice has (three) Advocates-General. This is a position unknown in America. The function of the Advocates-General is to act impartially to evaluate the law and facts of each case appearing before the court and to present their opinions to the court in the interests of justice. Their findings are not binding; but their influence is great. They are a permanent and institutionalized "amicie curiae" (Friends of the Court), bound to defend the law itself without fear or favor.

EEC policy towards business

Common Market competition Law is primarily designed to create an international market by breaking down national barriers.

The EEC is developing its own anti-trust merger and acquisition rules. Merely restricting the activities of large companies is not considered adequate.

Since "dumping" (the practice of releasing large quantities of excess goods into a foreign market at low prices for quick sale to reduce inventories) is prohibited within the free market of the EEC, this can create some serious problems for both home based EEC companies and foreign owned companies within the EEC.

The power to administer competition rules is given to the Commission. The main competition rules are Articles 85 and 86 of the Treaty of Rome.

The first (85) of these prohibits cartels (manufacturers' unions to control markets, prices and manufacturing of goods) and makes them, and other practices in restraint of trade, null and void. The Commission can make exceptions to this rule if it sees fit to do so.

The second (86) restrains private monopolies and near monopolies from abusing their power and influence in the market place.

The Commission has enforced Article 85 very strictly and has been lenient about Article 86.

Since one of the aims of the Common Market is to help European companies compete with large American companies, mergers within the EEC are to be encouraged in principle. That is why Article 86 has not been heavily enforced.

Under Article 86 the Commission can only take action where one party to a merger already has a "dominant position" in the market.

While Article 85 of the Treaty of Rome prohibits *large* concerns from combining both production and supply activities—small concerns are now encouraged to share these facilities in order to compete with larger companies. It is expected that joint research and development activities for small companies will also be exempted from the restrictions of Article 85 by order of the Commission.

Under the authority of Article 86 of the Treaty, a U.S. company, Commercial Solvents, has been fined and ordered to sell certain chemicals to a company competing with an Italian subsidiary of Commercial Solvents. The Court of Justice ruled that Commercial Solvents had abused its "dominant position" in the market. The Court in this case did not permit attempts at delaying tactics to succeed.

One aspect of the Commercial Solvents case may have effects outside the EEC itself. That is the contention that extra-territorial action which affects trade within the EEC is subject to EEC anti-trust regulations. This could cause great concern to some large multinational companies in the U.S.A.

There is unhappiness in some U.S. circles over a Court ruling in a Continental Can case. Here the court effectively rewrote Article 86 of the Treaty of Rome which forbids the abusive exploitation of a "dominant position" in any market if it affects trade between member states. In this case the Court ruled in effect that a company may not become so large that its competitors are unable to operate without being affected by it. So a company doesn't have to try to harm its competitors. Mere growth might be enough to make it guilty of violating the law.

In December 1973, the European Commission approved the merger of two German steel companies (already approved in Germany) but compelled one of the companies to divest itself of an interest in a third German steel company. Germany had imposed no such restrictions.

In America, anti-trust laws and their enforcement are extensive and are concerned more with substance and effect than with form. The United States seeks to control activities of companies—both foreign and domestic—which the Department of Justice believes will have an adverse effect on trade within the United States. (Action is taken even though the suspect activity takes place outside of the United States; although recent rulings have restricted such action.)

The EEC will lean heavily on the American experience in developing its own anti-trust legislation.

While European trade is becoming integrated rapidly, inter-European mergers have not caught on as they must in time. National laws still favor national mergers.

Italy has no anti-trust law while Belgium and Luxembourg hardly use theirs; and most of the other EEC countries' laws are much more concerned with prices than competition.

The only Common Market country with effective controls over mergers is Germany. In Germany the anti-trust laws require notification of mergers involving possible control of 20% or more of a market, or more than 10,000 employees; or an annual turnover of 50 million deutschmarks. Much of the present thinking about EEC merger regulations is based on the German model.

It is apparent that great concern exists within the EEC about

31

multinational companies, their capital movements, tax avoidance, production, inter-group trade, labor relations and export and import trade.

Proposed regulations to control mergers could have serious effects on companies whose activities extend outside the Common Market. Consequently, lawyers and other interested parties are following these proposals closely.

The EEC Code for Multinationals will probably include the following:—

1. A good conduct code for takeover bids requiring full disclosure of the details of an offer including the source of the purchase money. (Banks will not be used to hide the identity of the bidder as is often the case today.)

2. Inter-governmental cooperation to stop tax evasion and price cheating on inter-company sales and licensing agreements.

3. Publication of consolidated company accounts broken down by country showing details of investment funds, taxes, profits, sales, research costs and licensing income.

4. Most large scale dismissals of employees will be regulated.

5. Prior notice of mergers will be required.

6. Other regulations on international mergers, tax evasion, labor, capital movements and publication of information on multinational activities, as well as provisions for increased worker participation in company management, can be expected. These rules will probably apply to mergers involving a joint turnover of $200 million or more.

The EEC rules for European multinationals may well provide that their expansion into the Third World be done in a manner which will not upset local economics. This would put them at a disadvantage with their non-European multinational competitors.

The Commission has not yet worked out its policy regarding licensing and distribution agreements. Generally they do not like agreements which discriminate against certain distributors, wholesalers and retailers; but they do allow reasonable and non-arbitrary standards and conditions to be established by manufacturers.

In the course of time most restrictions will be lifted between Common Market countries. We can then expect a tightening of laws regarding outsiders. (We believe this will come through Articles 55 and 56 of the Treaty of Rome which gives member states the right to pass laws restricting the rights of foreigners for the public good.) However, at present, a foreign company, which establishes a branch or subsidiary in the EEC, can enjoy all the benefits of EEC membership through its branch or subsidiary.

Finance

The Common Market Council approved an EEC budget for 1974 of
five billion "units of account".

The unit of account is established by the Treaty of Rome as the
basis of settlement of financial obligations within and outside the EEC.
It provides a stable payment figure in spite of revaluations of
individual currencies. Each unit of account (U.A.) has 0.88867988 grams
of gold. It was equal to the value of one U.S. dollar in 1934 (the good
gold days). The value jumped under the "Smithsonian Agreement" of
1971, which changed the value of gold from $35 per ounce to $42.20.
Today with "the lid off" the price of gold, its value will undoubtedly
go up; but its basis for EEC purposes in 1974 is the same as in 1958.

There are about ten different U.A.'s in use today. These provide
temporary minor variations on the main theme to accomodate special
situations (the budget, coal and steel, Customs and others).

By January 1, 1975 the Community should be self-supporting. Its
revenue will come from levies, duties and VAT (Value Added Tax).

By 1980 the EEC intends complete monetary union. This means that
all its member nations' reserves will be pooled and probably some
degree of common currency.

The wealth of the EEC is staggering and four-five times that of the
U.S.A. in gold reserves.

Common Market Countries	Gold reserves in units of account based on Smithsonian values 1972
1. United Kingdom	4,478,000,000
2. France	8,183,000,000
3. Belgium 4. Luxembourg	2,627,000,000
5. Denmark	636,000,000
6. Ireland	957,000,000
7. Italy	4,903,000,000
8. Germany	18,920,000,000
9. Netherlands	3,219,000,000
TOTAL:	43,923,000,000

The EMCF (European Monetary Cooperation Fund) permits
central banks to borrow funds, during short term financial crises, up to

the following proposed amounts:

United Kingdom	600,000,000 U.A.
France	600,000,000 U.A.
Germany	600,000,000 U.A.
Italy	400,000,000 U.A.
Belgium	200,000,000 U.A.
Netherlands	200,000,000 U.A.
Denmark	90,000,000 U.A.
Ireland	35,000,000 U.A.

A further 1,500,000,000 U.A. is available to each country from the Community's central banks, at their discretion. The credits are for 3 months and are renewable. Each country contributes proportionately to the fund.

Under Article 129 of the Treaty of Rome, the European Investment Bank was established (EIB). It has a capital of 2,070,000,000 units of account. Twenty percent of the EIB's capital is subscribed for. The bank raises funds on the world's usual capital markets.

It lends those funds to promote Community projects, aid less developed regions of the EEC and to aid ventures between member states.

The seat of the bank is in Luxembourg. It is a very active financial institution.

Common Market Currency

The "Eurco" was created by the N. M. Rothschilds bank of England. Its aim is to eliminate both the borrowers and lenders exchange risks. Its value is not based on gold. It is a blend of all EEC currencies based on their GNP. The idea is that if some of the currencies go down in value, others will go up proportionately, thereby balancing it out. Perhaps one day this will be the Common Market currency.

A 15-year loan, underwritten by major European banks was made in 1973 with the U.S. dollar as the subscription unit, based on the value of the Eurco on the subscription date. The EIB will redeem the bonds before maturity. The bond is listed on the Luxembourg Stock Exchange and the Eurco value can be found daily in the Herald Tribune.

The value of the Eurco is the sum of its components: The Eurco is 28.9% Deutschmarks, 23.3% French Francs, 14.6% Pounds Sterling, 9.9% Italian Lira, 10.1% Dutch Guilders, 9.5% Belgian Francs, 2.7% Danish Krone, and 1% Irish Pounds. In November, 1973 one Eurco was worth about $1.26.

Regional Policy

The EEC is divided into 67 regions.

Whenever there is an imbalance in unemployment, a decline in GNP per capita, or a high rate of migration, aid is provided by the Community. The premise is that if any one country or region fell too far behind it could jeopardize the entire Community.

The Common Market Regional Fund for 1974 should be about 2½ billion dollars.

Great Britain, Italy and Ireland have the biggest regional problem areas in the EEC today.

Britain is counting heavily on a large regional fund. She is supported by Italy and Ireland—the other "have nots" of the EEC. Germany, the most prosperous of the nine, wants a small fund as she knows she will pay for most of it. She is supported by Holland and Belgium. They want to tie the Regional Fund to a Common Market energy policy in which Britain will agree to share her North Sea oil. How this question is resolved will influence Common Market policy and strength for years to come. Agreement was not yet reached in 1973 and early 1974.

Social Fund

During 1973, the Commission approved credits of about 185 million units of account for the European Social Fund. This fund was established primarily to provide assistance for retraining workers and secondly to help solve regional industrial problems.

The U.K. was the largest beneficiary of this fund, ($60 million) in its first year of membership.

Energy

Like the rest of the world the Common Market was caught off guard by the Arab oil cut-back; the total embargo on Holland; and the price increases.

While the Commission has tried for years to develop an energy policy for the EEC, the Council has not concluded a real policy but the 1973-1974 oil crisis has provoked a sense of urgency.

Holland is demanding that the EEC pool its resources. She is supported by Italy, Germany and the Benelux countries.

Most EEC oil is refined in Rotterdam. But England and France do not wish to anger the Arab oil producers who regard those two countries as "friends" and have taken less of a community approach to the problem.

England, and to a lesser extent, Denmark, Ireland and Italy are the only significant potential oil producers in the Common Market. They do not produce enough for their own needs at the present, let alone the others, although Britain hopes, with apparent justification, to be self-sufficient by 1980. Norway is the sleeping oil giant of the North.

35

Regional units of the European Community

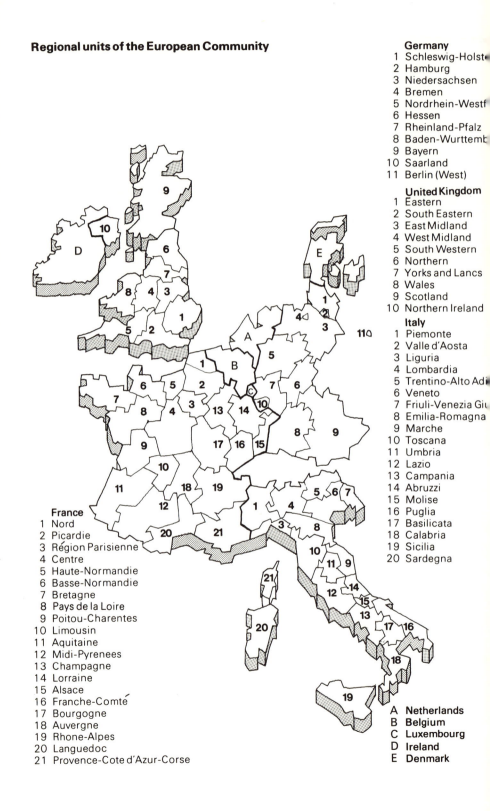

Germany
1. Schleswig-Holst⟨
2. Hamburg
3. Niedersachsen
4. Bremen
5. Nordrhein-Westf⟨
6. Hessen
7. Rheinland-Pfalz
8. Baden-Wurttemb⟨
9. Bayern
10. Saarland
11. Berlin (West)

United Kingdom
1. Eastern
2. South Eastern
3. East Midland
4. West Midland
5. South Western
6. Northern
7. Yorks and Lancs
8. Wales
9. Scotland
10. Northern Ireland

Italy
1. Piemonte
2. Valle d'Aosta
3. Liguria
4. Lombardia
5. Trentino-Alto Ad⟨
6. Veneto
7. Friuli-Venezia Gi⟨
8. Emilia-Romagna
9. Marche
10. Toscana
11. Umbria
12. Lazio
13. Campania
14. Abruzzi
15. Molise
16. Puglia
17. Basilicata
18. Calabria
19. Sicilia
20. Sardegna

France
1. Nord
2. Picardie
3. Région Parisienne
4. Centre
5. Haute-Normandie
6. Basse-Normandie
7. Bretagne
8. Pays de la Loire
9. Poitou-Charentes
10. Limousin
11. Aquitaine
12. Midi-Pyrenees
13. Champagne
14. Lorraine
15. Alsace
16. Franche-Comté
17. Bourgogne
18. Auvergne
19. Rhone-Alpes
20. Languedoc
21. Provence-Cote d'Azur-Corse

A **Netherlands**
B **Belgium**
C **Luxembourg**
D **Ireland**
E **Denmark**

Major community centres

Reykjavik
Iceland

Oslo
Norway

Copenhagen
Denmark

Amsterdam
Netherlands

Dublin
eland

London
Kingdom

Brussels
Belgium

Paris
France

Luxembourg
Luxembourg

Bern
Switzerland

Bonn

Germany

Prague
Czechoslovakia

Warsaw
Poland

Helsinki
Finland

Stockholm
Sweden
East Berlin
Germany

Vienna
Austria

Budapest
Hungary

Bucharest
Rumania

Belgrade
Yugoslavia

Sofia
Bulgaria

Madrid
Spain

Rome
Italy

sbon
ortugal

Tirana
Albania

Athens
Greece

© DIAGRAM

Much of her North Sea oil is unexplored as Norway has a stable, planned economy and a huge effort at oil production would upset its social order. Geologists feel that Norway's oil reserves are enormous.

England and Germany have sufficient coal reserves to be self-sufficient; but the other member states have declining reserves. Coal at present supplies less than 30% of Europe's energy requirements.

Another source of energy is natural gas. With large supplies in Holland and the North Sea, the Common Market might raise up to 20% of its energy needs from gas in ten years (in 1974 it is about 9%).

Nuclear energy is another hope for the future, but the huge costs and time factors do not offer any immediate promise.

Oil is still the key fuel for at least the next 15 years for about 50% of Europe's needs. This will mean balance of payments deficits for the EEC (at least until full North Sea production in 1980), which must import oil at ever increasing prices unless a new economic strategy can be developed.

While each nation struggles with its "personal" problems resulting from the energy crunch, ultimately they would appear to have no choice other than mutual assistance and cooperation.

The Council has ordered the Commission to draw up a "balance sheet" of EEC energy resources and thereafter proposals will be made for harmonizing national policies with EEC policies to develop a Common Market energy program for the future.

The EEC has called upon oil companies to give full information about their distribution procedures and policies. Since most of these companies are under American control, new rules on distribution of oil could affect U.S. supplies.

Insurance

Non-life insurance companies seeking to do business in the EEC must conform to rules regarding solvency, disclosure of risks covered, premiums, and re-insurance. (Premiums, incidentally, are heavily taxed on the continent, but are tax-free in the U.K.) In the EEC, the weaker party to a contract generally has the choice of court in which he will sue. Thus foreign insurance companies doing business in the EEC might be subjected to law suits where they least expect them.

There seems to be more litigation over insurance claims on the Continent than there is in England where there is less Government control. Perhaps this is due to the fact that British non-life insurance business is mainly international in scope (60%) rather than national as is the case on the Continent.

Until now, in Germany, it has been up to the Federal government to determine whether or not it wishes to grant access to the insurance market to foreigners. Belgium requires the issuance of a "carte professional". France requires more from foreign insurance companies than it does from French companies. Ireland requires that the shares of an insurance company be owned by Irish citizens and that a majority of board members be Irish.

Non-EEC insurance companies in addition to meeting the requirements of the governments under which they operate must keep to the following standards:

1. Be licensed to do business in their home country.
2. Keep separate records and accounts at each branch office.
3. Maintain proper solvency margins.
4. Get approval of the agent of their choice from each EEC country in which they operate.
5. Maintain proper reserves.
6. Keep, within the country in which they operate, assets equal to their required reserves in that country.

Provisions for life insurance companies are in the works. Probably they will require life and non-life insurance activities to be completely divided. This is done in Italy. France, Denmark, Germany, Holland and Ireland have "specialized" systems. But Britain, Belgium and Luxembourg have integrated systems which would have to be completely separated if these rules came into effect.

Patents and Trademarks

A new European patent law is being implemented to which 21 nations (including all EEC countries) have subscribed.

Under the "Europatent" system, an inventor can select the country(s) of his choice with Munich as the central office for all countries. Under a second convention in the Spring of 1974, a patent in any EEC country will be a patent in all EEC countries. Such patents will have to be translated into all EEC languages.

The new system will go into effect in 1977 and will run parallel to national systems for 10-15 years to allow for an orderly transition.

A 16 year patent should cost about $7,100 and a 20 year patent about $12,500.

Patents will be harder (and more expensive) to get because they will have to possess "inventive merit".

It is interesting that in Western Europe most patents are requested by foreigners (mainly Americans). Clearly many American inventors and patent holders will be affected by these new laws.

A trademark convention is being prepared to make uniform the EEC laws on this subject.

Transportation

Transportation together with agriculture and external trade is one of 39

Library of

Davidson College

three common policies specifically mentioned in the Treaty of Rome. Yet no common policy exists in this area. There is evidence that this is changing.

The Council has pledged to issue proposals in this area shortly.

A) Planes

As a result of inflation and the recent prosperity of Europe, the cost of manufacturing is rising more rapidly there than it is in America. Faced with currency revaluations many European companies find they cannot compete readily with their American counterparts. Take the aircraft industry by way of example.

European companies have lost between 20% to 35% of their business to U.S. companies.

In December, 1973, 74% of all airlines used in Europe were U.S. built (on a world-wide basis the figure was 90%). The fuel crisis will not inspire companies to switch to new and more expensive planes. It is predicted that by 1975 only 24% of aircraft flown in Europe will be of European origin (down from 30% in 1965).

Sabena Airlines (Belgium) recently ordered Boeing 737s to replace French Caravelles.

The Common Market Commission is cooperating with 11 European aircraft manufacturers to create an economic environment for survival of the industry. They propose establishment of the European equivalent to a CAB (Civil Aeronautics Board); an FAA (Federal Aviation Authority); standardization of credit, insurance, marketing and taxes, as well as a "buy European" campaign.

B) Ships

One of the major contributions the three new members made to the EEC was in the area of shipping.

It has been estimated that the amount of cargo handled by all of the seaports of all present EEC countries in 1972 was half of the world's total.

Also in 1972, the EEC had about 11% of the world's merchant marine fleet (tonnage-wise); with the addition of Great Britain, Ireland and Denmark they now have 24%. This gives the EEC the most significant merchant marine fleet in the world.

England has the largest fleet in the world, after Japan and Liberia (mainly U.S. controlled) and the most international in the EEC. Most of the other EEC nations use their ships primarily for national needs. Consequently, until recently there has not been much effort towards a shipping policy for the Common Market.

While estimates vary, Japan has about 45% of the world's shipbuilding capacity and orders. It is also estimated that by 1980 world capacity will be twice as much as will be required to fill demand. All the more reason to unite in order to survive and compete with the Japanese who are forging ahead to increase their capacity.

Within the last few years an interest in the tax advantages of ship ownership caused many American banks to open offices in London to compete with European banks for ship finance business. Until the Arab-Israeli war of 1973 the world's increasing demand for oil gave a strong impetus to ship construction.

The Commission has launched a campaign to rejuvenate European shipbuilding. The resources of the European Investment Bank, the Social Fund and the Regional Fund would be used to aid the industry. Whether or not the loss of oil tanker business resulting from the Arab oil crisis will change the need for this drive, or there will be a demand for nuclear-powered ships remains to be seen.

Space

The EEC does have a space program. In conjunction with the U.S.A. it is developing a "Spacelab" at a cost of $325 million. Another $480 million is being spent on a rocket-launcher for EEC use, "The Ariana". Finally about $75 million will be spent on a maritime communications satellite called "Marots".

Agriculture

One area of great interest and concern in the EEC is the CAP (Common Agricultural Policy). It is one of the major accomplishments of the Common Market to date. The essence of the policy is to provide high market prices for agricultural foods in order to aid small farmers. This benefits countries such as France and Holland who are major exporters of agricultural goods. Britain and Germany are net importers of agricultural goods and consequently pay more to support the CAP than they get from it. The CAP has protected EEC farmers from foreign competition.

To complicate the matter further there are still border taxes imposed by some countries (particularly Germany) against imports from other EEC countries. Consequently, a uniform price structure does not exist within the Common Market. There are also differences in local tax regulations, distribution facilities, customs and promotion. The biggest factor in price differentials within the Common Market is local distribution. Price variances within the EEC—for the same products—can be 50% or more. However, these price differentials are to be eliminated under EEC and GATT rules.

Internal customs regulations are probably more restrictive in France than in any other EEC country where special permits are required to import items such as honey, fish and wine.

41

Such customs taxes could potentially disrupt the CAP, and with it adversely affect the growth and unity of the EEC. They are alien to the concept of a free trade area and are therefore not compatible with the idea of a Common Market. However, the high value of the Deutschmark combined with inflation put the German farmer at a competitive disadvantage. Germany will not change its policy until there is full monetary and economic union in the EEC. Probably the solution to the problem lies in subsidies directly to the farmers rather than in maintaining artificially high market prices which result in such fiascos as the EEC storing huge quantities of butter at high prices and then being forced to sell it to Russia at low prices to avoid storage costs. Steps are being taken to reduce the inequities of the system.

Between 1962 and 1970 France received almost $1 billion more from the EEC agricultural fund than it contributed, and Holland about $400 million, more than it contributed. They were the only net gainers. Germany alone paid out $800 million more than she received from the fund.

EEC Commercial Trends

There is the very real possibility that a new form of company—The Euro-company (Societas Europia)—will be authorized by the Council. This will eliminate the national requirements for company formation and provide an EEC standard acceptable by all EEC members and ruled by EEC law.

It is expected that the Societas Europia will come into effect in 1976 or 1977.

By 1975 the EEC hopes to have a standard 40 hour work week and by 1976 four weeks annual paid holiday throughout the Common Market.

By 1978 all countries should have complied with a directive making company directors personally liable for the acts of their companies.

The EEC is establishing a consumer advisory group. Under this program, protection against health and safety hazards will be provided; and, in addition, information on goods and services will be more complete and uniform.

As is the case in all bureaucracies there is a great deal of red tape, paperwork and regulation with the EEC. It is estimated that over 300 documents are printed every year covering the Community's minor legislation. It is not always easy to know what to do, let alone how to do it.

Information about the EEC can be obtained from The European Community Offices in Washington, D.C. and in EEC information offices in every Common Market capital city.

III A General Commercial picture

Forms of Business

Anyone doing business in Europe must understand the differences between the various forms of Common Market business enterprises. Like the song in "The Music Man", "Ya gotta know the territory."

What Americans call a corporation is a "company limited by shares" in England and Ireland. In England "corporation" usually refers to municipalities rather than businesses. English companies have the word "Limited" after their names. In France, Belgium and Luxembourg large companies are called Société Anonyme (S.A.). In Germany they are Atkiengesellschaft (A.G.), in Denmark an Aktieselskab (A/S) and in Italy, Società per Azioni (S.p.A.).

In England they usually do not use the term "stock" certificate, but rather "share" certificate. "Stock", in the United Kingdom, refers only to fully paid up shares, which, unlike shares, are transferable in any amount (including fractions of shares). "Stock" must be created out of the original share capital of the company by company resolution.

However, it does not end there. The European countries have small companies which do not have share certificates. They are known as "private companies".

Private companies in France are known as *Société à résponsabilité limitée* (S.A.R.L.); in Belgium as *Société de personnes a responsabilité limitée* (S.P.R.L.); *Gesellschaft mit beschrankter Hoftung* (GmbH) in Germany; and *Società a responsibilità limitada* (S.R.L.) in

Italy. They might be likened to a partnership or joint venture; but in a simple company form which gives their owners the usual corporate advantages. The nearest thing to a private company in the United States is a "Subchapter S" corporation, where a company elects to be treated as a partnership (for tax purposes). In short, you get the benefits of the company's limitation of liability; but have the flexibility of functioning as a partnership.

The equivalents of the American Certificate of Incorporation are: England and Ireland—Memorandum and Articles of Association.

France, Belgium and Luxembourg—*Statuts*

Germany—*Satzung*

Italy—*Statuo*

Netherlands—*Statuten or Statuts*

Denmark—*Stiftelsesoverenskomst*

A certificate of Incorporation in Europe refers to a piece of paper authenticating the existence of a company and not its constitution and by-laws.

A Board of Directors is called: *Consiglio di Amministrazione* in Italy; *Conseil d'Administration* in French speaking countries and *Verwaltungsrat* in Germany.

Directerus and *Direktoren* are managers rather than directors as we know them. English directors are the executives of their companies.

A conglomerate would be called a *Konzen* in Germany and a *Groupe de Societes* in France. The parent company would be the *Muttergesellschaft* or *Société-mère* respectively while their subsidiaries would be either *Tochtergesellschafts* or *filiale*.

In some countries, like Belgium, partnerships do not exist for certain forms of business activity, such as the practice of law; and joint ventures do not have the same meaning as they do in America.

When forming companies, the same general registration requirements exist in most countries. However, each nation has its own formalities which must be observed. One should be alert to three factors:

1. In certain countries no company can be formed without the approval of a court.

2. In most EEC countries, publication of the details of a new company is required. This takes time and money.

3. Many functions, normally ascribed to the lawyer or local government in the U.S.A. are the function of the notary. A notary is a much more important person on the Continent than he is in the U.S.A. or Britain.

While some countries, such as Germany, Italy and Holland, permit "one man" companies (after formation), most countries require at least two members or shareholders for a private limited liability

45

company and three or more for a company limited by shares. In many EEC countries, a public or "share issuing" company may have *no less than* seven members. In most countries, *private* companies have an upward limit of 50 members.

Minimum company capital requirements exist in countries such as France, Germany, and Italy. In England there is presently no minimum capital requirement but this is expected to change soon. Most countries have laws requiring incorporators to pay for a minimum of 20-25% of the value of the initial subscribed share capital of their companies. For a small business venture this may be a significant factor in determining where you will form your foreign subsidiary.

Share certificates may or may not be negotiable instruments in Europe (they are in the United States). You may not be able to compel a company to register you as the new owner of the shares you have paid for even if you have a shareholders or company formation agreement. Registration may depend on local law or the Board of Directors. This calls for great caution—particularly when acquiring a minority interest in a European company. Merely having the share certificates may not be enough. On the other hand there may be an advantage in being a minority shareholder of a foreign company as such companies may accumulate profits without subjecting American shareholders to tax on undeclared dividends.

Many companies in Europe issue bearer shares which are freely transferable and are not registered. This permits secrecy which is sometimes desired; but if you lose the certificate you're out of luck.

In some countries you must have local directors to run the company. There are nations where directors have much more personal liability for the misconduct of their companies than is usually the case in America. This trend is increasing. Very strict legislation along these lines is being prepared in England.

France and Germany started a trend towards a two-tiered board of directors. One board runs the company on a day to day basis and has worker representation. The other provides general guidance and direction and usually represents the owners of the company. This trend will continue and will probably broaden into required Common Market company practice.

Under American law agreements outside the authority of the company are not enforceable. Such agreements are called "ultra vires". Under the laws of most EEC nations, companies can be held to *ultra vires* agreements, improperly made by their officers, by a person who entered into the agreement in good faith—even if it was made before the company was incorporated.

46

Mergers and Acquisitions

While regulation of mergers and acquisitions is minimal compared to the U.S.A., each country does have its own rules which must be adhered to.

The Netherlands offers the best choice for successful merger or acquisition according to a recent study. This is due to the high level of business and political integrity. Denmark comes next, followed by Germany and Italy. Italy however, also offers the greatest opportunity for failure of all the EEC countries.

Business Taxes

In the United States, corporation tax is based on the "classical" system. The company pays a flat rate on profits whether retained or distributed (although there may be a surtax on retained profits in excess of $100,000). The shareholders pay the same rate on dividends as they do on their other income (with minor exceptions). In Europe this is not usually the case.

Under the "split" or dual rate system in Germany, distributed profits (dividends) are taxed at a rate lower than retained profits.

Britain and France have the "imputation" system and *avoir fiscal* respectively. This method gives the shareholders a measure of tax relief on dividends. This system will probably be adopted by all Common Market countries in time.

VAT

Value Added Tax (VAT) is Europe's answer to the sales tax. Most purchases carry VAT as do services (legal fees, insurance etc.). There is a system of refunds so the taxpayer does not pay tax on previously taxed items; but rather on the "value added" to the product by the current seller. The idea is to eliminate purchase and luxury taxes and reduce the chance of tax cheating. Each EEC country has its own rates of VAT. Certain items are exempt (usually food and newspapers) in some countries. Great Britain has the simplest VAT system. Essentially it is a flat 10%. In other countries it varies from product to product. The EEC will ultimately finance itself by receiving 1% of all VAT revenue. This will require harmonization of all EEC VAT systems.

The reason the French and Italians smoke those strong dark tobacco cigarettes has more to do with taxes than with taste. France and Italy impose higher taxes on tobacco than do other countries because they use a value added tax system. Therefore they use cheaper tobacco to keep costs down. The tobacco industry in those countries is state owned. The EEC is forcing the state cartels to permit competition from abroad.

47

More tax tips

Investors in foreign public companies must have some acquaintance with local tax laws. "Withholding of tax at source" legislation is common in the western world. A comparison of the existing English and French tax laws regarding dividends shows that the foreign investor in England winds up with more net income than he would in France assuming the same gross income. With proper use of the benfits of tax credits resulting from double tax treaties, an American investor may actually wind up with a larger net dividend after taxes than the initial dividend itself. (See the chapter on France under the section on personal income taxes for a fuller discussion of this subject.)

Interestingly enough, the EEC provides many "tax haven" advantages. Luxembourg is noted for its holding company tax avoidance features. There are about 4000 such companies there. The Netherlands, the Netherlands Antilles, Gibraltar and the Channel Islands can all provide tax advantages for foreign companies. Combined with facilities in tax havens outside the Common Market, international businessmen operating in the Common Market could take advantage of tax laws and avoid (to some extent) heavy taxation of their profits. Difficult as it may be to believe, because of favorable double tax treaty arrangements between Europe and America, investing in Europe can sometimes be more profitable on a net basis than investing in developing countries.

In Belgium, where one-third of the manufacturing activities are controlled by "multinationals", payments to foreign holding companies must be supported by proof of a valid business purpose. By the way, you can form a "headquarters" company in Belgium which will be free of tax. (See Chapter on Belgium).

Italy is revising its tax laws to permit investigators to obtain information from Italian banks about suspected tax evaders. This should have a dramatic impact on Italian business practices.

It is estimated that over the last several years at least $10 billion has been illegally exported from Italy to be put in Swiss and other foreign bank accounts to avoid the tax collector.

In 1974 Italy introduces a new tax system where four taxes replace 34 confusing tax regulations. Personal income tax will start at 10% on income up to 2 million lire ($3,200); will go up to 50% on 80 million lire, and rise to 72% on income in excess of 500 million lire (about $800,000). The system will be similar to that of the U.S.A., with statutory exemptions and withholding tax.

Local taxes to support local improvements will range from 8.9% to 14.7%.

VAT and stiffer deduction and collection rules will make up the rest of the tax revenue.

France is changing its tax laws to "share the wealth" more evenly. Along with Italy it is the only country without a payroll or "pay as you earn" (P.A.Y.E.) tax system. This system will probably be introduced by 1978. The tax rate on long term (ten years for real estate) capital gains will rise to 15%. Tax rates and allowances will also change in 1974 so the lower paid will pay less tax and the rich will pay more.

Wealthy people have often taken up residence in France to avoid taxes. France, being essentially a Latin country, has always had a casual attitude towards income taxes. Residents could often avoid tax altogether or "make a deal" with the local revenue agent. One's standard of living was often assessed on the amount of rent one paid, on the theory: high rent=high income. Now things are changing and the government is cracking down on the rich—the recent case of Mr. Wildenstein being the most sensational.

Holland will soon raise its property, inheritance and automobile taxes.

Money

Each member state has its own currency. Each currency has its own value. If you are doing business in the EEC you must know these currencies and their values. They can be found listed in the Financial Times, The Herald Tribune and the Wall Street Journal daily.

Much must be done before a CMP (Common Monetary Policy) is agreed within the EEC. However, one day there most probably will be one currency for all those countries, and one central bank to handle all of the community's reserves.

Anyone establishing a business in an EEC country should check on the financial resources available to him.

Is local capital available? If so, on what terms? Are there exchange control regulations? Free movement of capital is one of the major goals of the EEC financial policy. Local exchange control regulations will eventually give way; but this has not yet come to pass. Even when it does come into effect, the problem of moving funds out of the EEC will undoubtedly remain. The member nations do restrict currency movements in times of fiscal emergency. Italy, France and England are particularly sensitive about abuses of their exchange control regulations. It is a very serious matter to violate exchange control regulations.

Distribution vs Agency Agreements

It is essential to know the effects of the selection of various forms of doing business in Europe. Distribution and agency agreements are a prime example of this problem. The title you give an agreement will

49

not determine what it is in the eyes of a foreign court. In Europe, agency agreements may subject you to excessive tax liability; whereas distribution agreements may give you more protection. Consult counsel before deciding which is best for you as there is no simple rule to cover all cases.

Accounting

New Common Market accounting as well as pricing, credit, insurance, banking, company law, payroll and tax regulations must also come into effect to harmonize and facilitate business growth within the Common Market.

There are widely varied accounting and bookkeeping practices in the nine Common Market countries. No one in France or Italy would accept the books of a company as truly reflecting its financial position. The books are for the tax collector. Often there is another set of books for the owners and sometimes a third set for a prospective purchaser or a partner. Tax avoidance is almost a way of life in France and Italy.

Accounting practices on the Continent are more closely regulated (but in narrow areas) than in the U.K.—where tradition and honor are significant influences. But no where is it as regulated as in the U.S.A.— as an example—the SEC (Securities and Exchange Commission) regulations on disclosures.

However, there is a definite trend in Europe, due largely to workers participation in management, (such as the Works Council in Holland) for fuller disclosures of business accounts.

In England accountants take the place of company and tax lawyers to a great extent. This is not usually the case in the rest of the Common Market.

In Britain balance sheets are designed to show net assets, shareholders equity and employment of funds. On the Continent it is usual to only show total assets and liabilities. Each country has its own rules for company accounts. Reserves are an important balance sheet item in Continental accounts and a trap for the unwary. Depreciation rules vary markedly within the EEC. Group consolidated accounts are not required—outside of Britain—and are infrequently provided. In Germany consolidated reports are required only for domestic subsidiaries.

In Belgium, where there are less than 500 public companies, there is little stimulus for sophisticated accounting and reporting procedures. The law requires little, and little is revealed that is not required by tax and company law.

While France boasts the second largest number of companies in the EEC (250,000), most of them are small family businesses. Consequently, France has not given much importance to accounting; and the government has involved itself in the profession thus inhibiting development within the profession. Accounts in France generally are incomplete, unconsolidated and often misleading (for reasons of privacy and tax avoidance). When French companies seek listing on the London Stock Exchange they usually use British accountants. By law, some parts of French accounts are quite detailed. Reserves must be maintained and depreciation must be strictly accounted for. A French accountant is called an *Expert Comptable* (roughly equivalent to the U.S.—C.P.A.) and an ordinary accountant a *Comptable Agrée*.

Accelerated depreciation is available in Germany in special cases (to fight pollution among others) up to 80% and in the U.K. up to 100% for investments in development areas.

Labor

In 1971 approximately 18% of the working population of the Common Market countries was self-employed—as compared with 11% in the U.S.A.

Germany has about 2½ million foreign (non EEC country) workers while France has about 1½ million.

It was estimated that more than 11 million foreign workers will have to be integrated into Europe in order to maintain a 6% annual growth rate. This creates a range of social and labor problems for the host countries. France is now already confronting serious problems with its primarily African foreign workers.

The Dutch with only 150,000 foreign workers have bad social relationships with those workers and restrict their entry.

As a result of the oil crisis, Germany has restricted the entry of more foreign workers. During recessive economic periods in the EEC the economies of countries such as Yugoslavia, Turkey and Greece are hurt by the loss of income being sent home by their nationals working in the EEC.

Britain, Italy and Ireland are the only net losers of labor in the EEC. They also happen to be the countries with the lowest average pay scales. Workers in the North of England, Scotland and Wales are the poorest paid in the Common Market, averaging 25% less than their continental colleagues.

Thirty-five per cent of the needy people in the EEC live in Italy, 25% in Great Britain, 21% in France, 9% in Germany, 4% in Ireland and the balance divided mainly between Holland and Belgium.

The European Social Fund provides training and re-training programs for idle and unskilled labor. The Fund has about $225 million for use among the nine. Company programs are eligible for these funds as well as governmental or industrial board programs. Fund rules also provide that the Fund will match contributions by a

51

government to a private training program. Foreign companies can take advantage of these funds when setting up in Europe.

There is a secretarial shortage in Europe, particularly of multilingual secretaries. In general they earn less than their American counterparts, but get more vacation and social security benefits.

Unions

Ford workers in Britain and West Germany agreed to make joint demands for vacations, a shorter work week, reduction of overtime and reduction of stress on the shop floor. It is easy to see how this concept will spread to the point of international strikes.

In Germany there is a system of one union per plant rather than a union for every catagory of labor. In other countries unions are founded on an industrial or religious basis.

Employment

It is important to know the rules regarding work permits, as well as local regulations and business practices regarding social security, pension and profit sharing plans, insurance and other fringe benefits. Citizens of countries outside the Common Market may have difficulty in gaining entry to or employment in the EEC. EEC nationals have the right to live and work where they please within the Common Market.

Employees living in countries having strong social security and employment laws (such as France and Belgium), who work and travel abroad can suffer large losses of real income, as a result of loss of benefits available only to residents. In such cases, the employer may be forced to give pay supplements to compensate for these losses. One might employ executives in low tax areas and provide them with suitable pension and health plans. They could then work for subsidiaries of the parent company—each of which would be charged by the parent for the value of services rendered to them by the executive. In this way foreign employers might avoid some of the problems of executive recruitment in the EEC.

In Germany one can give paid vacations to executives without increasing their taxable income.

In Holland and Britain, as in the U.S.A., most pension plans are fully funded. In France they work on a "pay as you go" basis. In Germany, the employer-company is permitted to invest pension funds in the company itself. The company could fail—with a consequent loss of workers' benefits.

In Belgium, Italy and Holland, it can prove to be very expensive to fire someone or go out of business. Severance pay requirements are excessive.

Dutch salesmen usually prefer to work under close supervision with relatively high pay and low commissions. Belgians, on the the other hand tend to be more individualistic and motivated more by a high commission—low salary system. Belgians are less inclined to want their employment agreements to be in writing.

Rents and Property

A comparison of office rents in Europe will show that London is the most expensive city (in terms of rents) and Belgium offers the best rental values. Britain's stringent zoning and building laws prevent both the destruction of historic buildings and the construction of high rise offices. The British have developed property on the Continent more than any other nation. It is estimated that 75% of prime Brussels office space is British owned.

Property developed in Germany has to a large extent been controlled by local banks or "closed end" investment funds also under the control of banks. Consequently, the market is generally not open to the property developer.

It is estimated that 50% of all property in the Alsace Lorraine section of France are sales to Germans. Land prices have risen 700% in ten years.

Property development in France is highly regulated; but very profitable once in operation.

France has imposed severe restrictions on land hoarding and office developments in Paris in an effort to drive property companies away. This is due in no small measure to foreign (mainly British) developers who have exploited the Paris property market. British investment in French property is estimated at $1\frac{1}{2}$ billion dollars and rising. (Their total European property investment is estimated at $12 billion.) Prime office rents in Paris are now sometimes $25 a foot and increasing.

The British seem to be concentrating on France for their European business activities. In the first half of 1973, 52 out of 150 European acquisitions by British companies were made in France (according to the London Chamber of Commerce). There were 42 made in the Netherlands. Property and construction led the field.

Home Loans

The Dutch generally can get 90% house mortgages with payments over 30 years. The same can be the case in England; but interest rates and the cost of property are high in England. The French usually can get no more than 75% mortgages repayable in 15 years. In addition, notarial and surveyors fees can add 10% to the cost of property.

In Germany the *Bausparkassin* have a scheme similar to the British Building Societies where young people can save and get priority for home loans on favorable terms. In Germany supplemental finance is

53

also available. In Belgium loans used to be for only 60% of the house value repayable in 20 years and Belgians traditionally prefer to rent rather than to buy; but there is a trend to purchasing with the introduction of better financial terms. Italy provides state aid for housing for up to 75% of cost; but private homes usually merit only 50% mortgages repayable within 25 years.

Market Testing

Belgium is considered to be the home of Mr. Average European. It is centrally located and probably the best place to test-market products. Its import-export regulations are the easiest in Europe and its facilities the least expensive. Belgians enjoy their food and are reputed to be the largest drinkers of beer per capita in the world. (Although the Bavarians hold the record as a region and Italians are the largest wine drinkers).

The Metric System

We live in a changing world. Feet into metres; Fahrenheit to Centigrade; gallons to litres and pounds to kilos. Essentially, it's the good old decimal system with a continental accent. The following examples may help one to "cope".

Instead of pints, quarts and gallons most Europeans use litres. The symbol for litre is L. One litre equals about $1\frac{3}{4}$ pints, $4\frac{1}{2}$ L = approximately 1 gallon.

Instead of Fahrenheit, Centigrade is the measure of temperature in Europe. Freezing is 0°C (32°F), while boiling temperature is 100°C (212°F). The formula for conversion is $F = \frac{9}{5}C + 32°$ or $C = \frac{5}{9}F - 32°$. Normal body temperature is 37°C.

There are about 38 grammes to the ounce and a kilogramme is about 2.2 pounds. A metric ton is a bit less than a U.S. ton.

There are about $2\frac{1}{2}$ centimetres to the inch. A metre is a bit more than 3′3″ and a kilometre is a bit more than $\frac{6}{10}$ of a mile.

There is a variance in clothing sizes between the U.S.A., England and the Continent.

Travel

Duty free allowances are being phased out within the Community within the next three years. They will remain for foreigners and for travel outside the Common Market.

Free Medical Care

Europeans are proud of their National Health plans. Residents of the Common Market are entitled to the same medical treatment as the natives of any other Common Market country in which they are travelling. In Britain, Ireland, Italy, Denmark, Holland and Germany this can mean free treatment; whereas in France, Belgium and Luxembourg it means substantial savings. In Britain, treatment is free for all people, including visitors.

EEC citizens intending to visit another Community country obtain the proper application form from their local Department of Health and Social Security Office. Having completed this, they receive form E111 entitling them to medical benefits in other Community countries.

Procedures for obtaining benefits vary from country to country. The general rules are as follows:

Belgium: Doctors' fees and the cost of medicine must be paid in full: but on presentation of a health form and the receipted bill at the local social security office at least 75% of these expenses are refunded. A substantial part of hospital fees can be recovered in the same way.

Denmark: Free medical treatment is provided on presentation of a passport and the doctor arranges for free hospitalization if necessary. Prescriptions are available at reduced rates, and visitors can recover most dental fees for urgent treatment.

France: Before seeing a French doctor, visitors obtain a form from their local social security or health office. This form (*feuille de maladie*) entitles them to a refund of 70% of the doctor's fees and between 70% and 90% of the cost of medicine. Eighty per cent of the cost of hospital treatment is met by the local social security office. Surgical treatment is paid in full.

Germany: By presenting the proper form at the local sickness insurance office (*Allgemeine Ortskrankenkasse*) the visitor receives a sickness document (*Krankenschein*) and a list of doctors and dentists in the insurance scheme. Free treatment is given, although there is a standard charge for prescriptions. A similar procedure entitles the traveller to free hospital service.

Ireland: Arrangements are the same as for Denmark. It should be made clear by applicants they wish to have such treatment under European Community rules.

Italy: Visitors presnt their form to the local sickness insurance office (*Institute Nazionale per l'Assicurazione control delle Malattie—INAM*) and receive a certificate and a list of doctors in the scheme. The certificate entitles them to free treatment by a doctor. Some medicines are free; for others a small charge is made. Hospitals with an arrangement with INAM provide free service.

Luxembourg: Sickness offices issue sickness documents on presentation of the proper form. Visitors have to pay doctors' and dentists' bills, but will be reimbursed for all treatment and for most of the cost of medicine. Hospital treatment is normally free.

Netherlands: Doctors' and dentists' fees, and the cost of medicines

55

and hospital treatment are payable directly by the authorities with no charge to the visitor on presentation of his form.

The nine member countries of the EEC are still very much individual nations in terms of their customs, practices, and regulations in all fields and respects. The Common Market influence and direction towards harmonization is, however, already having its impact. The trend towards unification and harmony is the path of the future.

IV BELGIUM

Belgium

ROYAUME DE BELGIQUE

1 2 3
1 black
2 yellow
3 red

Total population 9,695,379

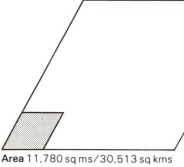

Area 11,780 sq ms/30,513 sq kms

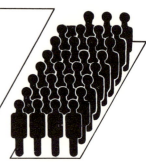

Population density 823 per sq m/318 per sq km

Form of government Constitutional monarchy. Executive power is exercised by the Monarch, Government, and Prime Minister. Legislative power is vested in the Monarch, the Government, and the Parliament, comprising the House of Representatives and the Senate. Election to the House of Representatives is by direct, proportional, compulsory, and universal suffrage. Election to the Senate is both direct and indirect and is for a 4-year term.

Head of state The Monarch/hereditary succession

Voting age 21 years

Public health Compulsory contributory state insurance

Major imports Raw materials, minerals, non-precious metals, machinery

Major exports Steel, textiles, machinery, chemicals, pharmaceutical products

Currency Belgian franc

50	100	150m
100	200km	

ercantile marine 89
ssels / 1,076,330 grt (1972)

litary personnel 96,000

ficial language(s) Flemish,
ench, German

hool-leaving age 14 years

gher education 14
stitutes / 75,106 places

embership of international
ganisations OECD, EEC,
uncil of Europe, Benelux,
e UN and its agencies

If it's Tuesday it must be . . .

Introduction

Belgium is a small, properous and strategically located country. Many think it is the best place to eat in the world. Antwerp is the world's third largest port (after Rotterdam and New York). The capital, Brussels is the main headquarters for Common Market administrative agencies and the home of NATO.

Belgium's population is about 10 million. About 50% of Belgians are Flemish (Dutch)-speaking and live mainly in the northern part of the country. Approximately one-third of the country is *Walloon*. They speak French and live primarily in the south. Both languages, and German, are official languages in Belgium. Both communities have very strong ethnic feelings which have led to many political crises in recent years. When doing business in Belgium you must be careful about language and ethnic factors.

Many Belgians are bi-lingual (more than 10% of the population have some knowledge of English) and have an ability to "understand" foreigners rivaled only by the Italians. There are a number of English schools.

Belgium has an area of 11,781 square miles. France is to the south, Germany and Luxembourg to the east, Holland to the north and the Atlantic Ocean to the west.

Belgium and Holland compete for the title of the most densely populated country in the world with Britain close behind.

Only 50% of Belgian land is suitable for farming but a high proportion (20%) consist of fine forests.

While not rich in raw materials Belgium does have significant deposits of coal and iron ore.

Most public utilities are government-owned (railroads, gas, electricity, post office, telephone and telegraph).

Belgium is highly industrialized. It relies on imports of raw materials, excellent communication and distribution systems and a skilled labor force to make its exports competitive. It is essentially a free enterprise society.

Belgium exports about 40% of its industrial production.

As an incentive to foreign investment Belgium provides capital grants. low interest rate loans and temporary exemptions from real estate taxes. Special grants are also available for training personnel for new industries.

Belgium has fewer import-export regulations than any other country and excellent warehousing and distribution facilities.

There are more investments in Belgium from U.S. business than from any other nation (about $30 billion) and the U.S. is its third largest trading partner.

Located at the heart of Western Europe, Belgium is considered by many large companies to be the best place to test market new products before moving into other European countries. Its advertising media are inexpensive and adaptable. It specializes in outdoor advertising.

Belgium uses the metric system.

Political Structure

Belgium is a constitutional monarchy. The monarch is head of state but rules through his ministers. There are 11 political parties which leads to political instability. Usually there is a coalition government.

The main source of law in Belgium is the Constitution. Only Parliament can interpret the Constitution, which is a very enlightened law. Parliament is divided into two houses: a Senate of 178 members (106 popularly elected, 48 appointed by the provincial councils and 24 by the senate itself); and a House of Representatives of 212 members. All serve four-year terms unless the coalition collapses (which is usually the case).

Legal System

Belgium has a civil law—a legal system similar to that of France, where statutes are the main source of law.

In addition to the Constitution, Belgium has civil, commercial and penal codees. The country is divided into nine provinces and a number of municipalities (*steden* and *gemeenten* in Dutch, and *villes* and *communes* in French) which have a great deal of power and autonomy.

Belgium has 222 judicial cantons, each with a justice of the peace. There are 26 judicial districts. In each district there is a district court, a court of first instance (this has civil, criminal and juvenile branches), a labor court and a commercial court. In the latter two courts some of the judges, by law, are laymen.

There are Courts of Appeal and above them the Supreme Court. The Supreme Court determines only law—not facts. If it reverses a lower court, the case is sent back for retrial. No court or judge is obliged to follow a ruling made by any other court or judge. The sole exception is where the Supreme Court has twice reversed the judgement of a lower court in a specific case. Then the Supreme Court's ruling becomes the law for that case only. As a practical matter, of course, courts do pay attention to the rulings of other courts.

Regardless of the provisions in an agreement, Belgian courts will apply Belgian law. Arbitration agreements will usually be upheld however.

No foreign judgment can be enforced in Belgium unless ratified by a Belgian court. There must be a full hearing on procedural and substantive issues. This position is modified by EEC rules and by treaties with a few other countries (but not the U.S.).

Hours of Business

Commercial establishments: 08:00 to 12:00 and 14:00 to 18:00 Monday to Friday.

Government offices: 09:00 to 12:00 and 14:00 to 17:00 Monday to Friday.

Banks: 09.00 to 12:00 and 14:00 to 16:30 Monday to Friday.

Vacations

There are 10 legal vacations in Belgium, these are:
New Year's Day
Easter Monday
Labor Day (May 1)
Ascension Day (40 days after Easter)
Whit Monday (Monday after Pentecost)
National Holiday (July 21)
Assumption (August 15)
All Saints' Day (November 1)
Armistice Day (November 11)
Christmas Day

Currency and Banking

The basic monetary unit is the franc (B.Fr.) divided into 100 centimes.

The government Banque Nationale de Belgique through the Commission Bancaire controls the domestic and foreign banks in Belgium. It can call for special deposits, impose ratios and other regulations.

Belgium offers a full range of banking services. Competition is keen.

There are many foreign banks in Belgium and all are required to maintain minimum amounts of capital. U.S. banks are well represented.

Exchange Control

Exchange Control regulations do not tend to be oppressive in

Belgium. However they are being tightened.

Investments do not require prior approval except where a large (over B.Fr. 100 million) or publicly traded Belgian company is being acquired.

Foreign capital may be freely imported and exported. Belgium maintains a two-tier currency system. The free exchange (financial franc) market is used for investments; the controlled exchange market (commercial franc) is for commercial transactions. You can however obtain guarantees from the Institute Belgo-Luxembourgois du Change (IBLC) that your money will be repatriated when you choose to export it back home.

Payments for exports must normally be received within six months and imports in three months.

Dividends, interest and royalties can be freely paid by Belgian companies to foreign nationals. The earnings of foreigners can be sent abroad.

Foreigners can borrow money locally.

The IBLC controls currency flows for both Belgium and Luxembourg. For all practical purposes the two currencies and the regulations controlling them are the same.

Forms of doing Business

Belgium permits the following types of business entities. (Since French names are used in the south and Flemish in the north, to avoid confusion only the English names will be used. See France and Holland respectively for proper names.)

1. *General partnership*

2. *Limited partnership*

3. *Limited partnerships with shares* (similar to a corporation; but there is no provision for limiting the liability of the general partners).

General and limited partnerships are formed by private or formally authenticated contracts.

4. *Cooperative companies.* These have variable capital and are used mainly by small businessmen wishing to pool their resources. Members can increase or decrease their contributions or retire from the company at any time.

5. *Private limited liability company*—a limited partnership in private corporate form with a minimum capital of B.Fr. 250,000 and a maximum membership of 50, none of whom may be companies. It may not do banking or insurance business. The transfer of its shares is restricted.

Limited partnerships with shares and private limited liability companies are formed by formal contracts, authenticated before a notary.

63

6. *Joint stock company*. This is most similar to a large U.S. company. The duration is only 30 years but this period is extendable indefinitely. These companies may be formed by public offer or, more usually, directly with at least seven initial founder shareholders.

Formation (Joint Stock Company)

A Belgian corporate charter is the equivalent of the certificate of incorporation and by-laws of a U.S. company. The founders must appear before a notary (all but one can appear by proxy) who authenticates and signs the charter together with the incorporators or their nominees. It is then registered, filed in the Commercial Register and published in the Official Gazette.

There is a tax of $2\frac{1}{2}\%$ on the *subscribed* capital and a statutory notarial fee depending on the amount of capital in the company. The rates start at .79% on the first B.Fr. 1 million of capital and decrease to .02% for over B.F. 107 million. The minimum fee is B.Fr. 500.

There is no minimum capital requirement. All of the capital must be subscribed for and at least 20% paid immediately. Payment may be in cash or in kind, including goodwill and know-how. If payment is not in cash the assets contributed must be listed and their value certified.

Shares and Shareholders

Shares may be owned by companies as well as individuals and by residents or non-residents.

A company cannot purchase its own shares unless it has a surplus over its capital and legal reseve requirements.

Shares may be issued with or without par value and may be in either bearer or registered form until they are fully paid. If the shares are not fully paid the company could refuse to transfer title to them on its books.

Beneficiary shares may be issued which do not represent invested capital. The rights of such shares are usually set out in a company's charter.

No shareholder may vote more than 20% of the total voting rights of a company or more than 40% of the votes at a shareholders' meeting.

Management

A minimum of three directors is required. There are no nationality requirements for directors. Directors serve for six years and, if foreign, must obtain a permit in order to do business in Belgium.

The operation of Belgian companies is similar to that of U.S. companies with the following exceptions:

1. Before any executive (or director) has the power to act as
corporate officers do in the U.S., the board of directors must delegate

such power to him and this authority must be published in the
Official Gazette.

2. The company's books and records must be periodically audited by
auditors (*commissaires* or *commissaressen*) who are elected for fixed terms
of no more than six years. In public companies at least one of these
auditors must be a Belgian qualified C.P.A. (although not necessarily
Belgian).

3. At least 5% of the company's net annual profit must be set aside
in a reserve until it equals 10% of the company's capital.

4. Within 30 days of approval by the shareholders, the company must
publish its annual balance sheet, profit and loss statement, the method
of distributing net profits, state of its capital (with a list of shareholders
who have not fully paid for their shares) and the names and addresses of
directors and auditors.

5. When changing the corporate charter or capital, or in order to
dissolve the company, special shareholders' meetings may have to be
held in the presence of a notary with larger quorum and voting
requirements than is usual.

6. If losses reach 75% of the initial capital of a company the
shareholders must meet to decide if the company should continue.

7. If losses equal the capital, the company must cease trading.

8. There are no laws about quorums.

Private Companies

The number of shareholders may range from 2 to 50. No
corporation may be a shareholder. There are restrictions on the transfer
of shares. All shares must be of the same class and have a minimum
value of B.Fr. 1,000.

Private companies may not enter the following fields: banking,
insurance and certain investment business.

The corporate charter need not be published and annual accounts
need not be filed. Therefore the costs of forming a private company are
lower than those of a joint stock company.

Alternatives to forming a new company exist. The following are four
possibilities:

Forms of Doing Business
Branches

Any company having its head office in Belgium is considered
Belgian even though it is incorporated elsewhere. For tax purposes
branches are regarded as separate entities from their parent companies.

To establish a branch you must file, with the registrar of a Belgian
commercial court, a copy of your Certificate of Incorporation and a
copy of a company resolution approving the opening of a Belgian

65

branch. These must be published in the annexes of the State Gazette (in Dutch or French depending on your location). Then you must register with the Register of Commerce, obtain a registration number, keep proper accounting records, designate a Belgian representative to be responsible for your taxes and provide a guaranty for payment of taxes. The guaranty must be equal to three times the estimated annual tax (minimum B.Fr. 10,000) and may be provided by a bank.

The cost of establishing a branch in Brussels would be about B.Fr. 5,000 plus legal fees.

Headquarters Office

It is possible to have a "headquarters" company office in Brussels to coordinate overseas activities of affiliates. Such companies may be classified as "non-earning" and therefore tax free. The main criterion is that such an office does not directly take or give sales orders.

Distributors

A distributor in Belgium is anybody buying or selling for his own account and who assumes all financial risks. By using a distributor you avoid doing business in Belgium. There is however a 7% tax on the importation of goods by Belgian distributors.

If the distribution agreements are exclusive and are for an *indefinite* period of time they may not be cancelled without adequate notice. Usually this means enough time to permit the other party to find a new principal or distributor. If the agreement is cancelled without the Belgian distributor having been guilty of a serious breach of the relationship, the principal may have to compensate the distributor for expenses incurred (sums he must pay to staff he discharged as a result of the loss of business and compensation for business lost).

Agents

Agency agreements fall into several categories:

1. Employment agreements which are governed by Belgian labor laws.

2. Principal and agent agreements where the agent is an independent person or company. Simple contract law prevails here.

3. General agents have the power to bind their principals.

4. Independent commission agents act in their own names for undisclosed principals.

5. Brokers and forwarders of orders have limited authority to act for their principals.

Taxation

Belgium's taxes are among the lowest in the Common Market.

The Belgian tax system is characterized by these features:

1. A single tax on total income.
2. Four categories of taxpayers each of whose income is subject to a single tax.
   a. individuals residing in Belgium;
   b. corporations and profit-making organizations;
   c. non-profit organizations;
   d. individuals or companies subject to the non-resident income tax.
3. A tax prepayment system exists where payments are credited against the tax due on the following year's income.

Company Tax

Corporations are taxed on their net profits whether or not distributed. The standard rate of corporate tax is 30% with the following variations on undistributed profits (which include reserves and non-deductible expenses):

1. On profits up to B.Fr. 1,000,000, the tax rate is 25%.
2. B.Fr. 1,000,000 to B.Fr. 1,250,000, the tax is 25% of the first B.Fr. 1,000,000 and 50% on the remainder.
· 3. On undistributed profits in excess of B.Fr. 1,250,000, the standard 30% rate is levied on the full amount.
4. In cases of undistributed profits in excess of B.Fr. 5 million, the rate increases to 35%. *This rate applies to profits of all foreign companies.*

Two additional surcharges of 10% are also levied. These are on the tax on taxable profits in excess of B.Fr. 3 million. This charge is limited so that it may not be greater than 20% of the taxable income over B.Fr. 3 million.

Corporations must also pay a municipal tax equal to 6% of the corporate tax imposed on Belgian income. (This is calculated on the basic tax rates.)

The "effective" rate of company tax is about 6% higher than the apparent "standard" rates.

Foreign companies pay a higher tax on their profits. (See point 4 above.)

Tax free reserves may be created for potential business losses. These must relate to itemized future risks rather than for losses in general. The amount of the reserves is limited to 5% of annual profits each year, and the cumulative reserve totals may not exceed 7.5% of the highest profit achieved in any of the proceding five years. There are also provisions for tax free reserves for future spending on building and and equipment and for special financial aid to employers.

Deductions

Generally Belgian income taxes, including provincial taxes, are not deductible from gross income. However, foreign taxes and Belgian taxes

67

levied on revenues other than income are deductible as expenses.

Interest payments are allowed as deductions so long as the withholding tax at source is retained and the rate is considered reasonable. The standard applied to test the reasonableness of the rates is that they be within 3% of the discount rate of Banque Nationale de Belgique.

Rents and royalty payments may be deducted from gross income.

Dividends between related companies qualify for a 95% tax exemption if received by an operating company; or 90% if received by a financial holding company. (The remaining 5% or 10% may be reduced by interest charges and general expenses.) Any balance remaining is subject to withholding tax.

Withholding Tax

Dividends received from foreign companies are subject to a 10% withholding tax. Some double tax treaties grant the option to Belgian companies of paying the standard .20% withholding tax rate on Belgian source dividends which are redistributed to shareholders and an exemption from the 10% tax on foreign source dividends.

The 10% withholding tax cannot be credited against corporate tax. However, 90% or 95% of the net dividend received is tax exempt if the applicable Belgian corporate rate is less than 30%.

The withholding tax on dividends, interest and royalties varies according to treaty. Dividends and interest paid to U.S. companies are subject to a 15% withholding tax while no tax is charged on royalties.

Most capital gains are taxed as ordinary income. Capital losses are fully deductible. Reduced tax rates of 15% apply to gains from the sale of land, buildings, equipment and securities held for a maximum of five years. Unrealised capital gains are taxed at the 15% rate upon revaluation and when the resulting gain is entered in the company's profit and loss statement.

A foreign company is taxable on all income received or produced by its Belgian permanent establishments. A permanent establishment includes a place of management, a branch, factory, workshop, agencies, store, office or warehouse.

The foreign company must be careful to set up adequate bookkeeping procedures to avoid a tax assessment on assumed profit.

Company tax returns are to be filed within one month of the annual general meeting and no later than six months after the fiscal year ends.

Foreign companies without Belgian establishments are free of tax on income earned in Belgium, except to the extent such income is withheld at source (20%), is derived from property (usually 25%) or is subject to capital gains tax. Again double tax treaty arrangements may affect these rates.

Pre-Payments

There is one trap for the unwary. You must correctly estimate and prepay the tax within 15 days of the end of the first half of the year in which the income is earned. Failure to do so results in the tax being increased by 3.75% if paid up to three months late, 7.5% if paid within six months of the due date and 15% if paid after that.

Withholding tax on dividends, royalties and interest and on remuneration is due within 15 days of their payment. A penalty of 7.2% per year, or 0.67% each month is levied on late payments.

Personal Income Tax

Belgian residents are taxed on their world-wide income. As in the case with companies, income from property is based on the presumed income and must be prepaid. Such payments are credited against your income tax liability.

There are three categories of individual taxpayer:
1. Belgian residents who are taxed at normal rates,
2. Non-residents who qualify for a 50% income exemption, and
3. Non-residents who qualify for a 30% exemption on their income.

Non-residents are subject to income tax on their Belgian source income. The normal tests of residence are physical presence of the taxpayer and his family, employment in Belgium, maintenance of a home, and certain economic ties in Belgium.

There is special tax treatment granted to foreign employes of companies controlled from outside Belgium. A taxpayer that qualifies will only be subject to the non-resident income tax on his aggregate Belgium source income. The special tax privilege is only available to:
1. Foreigners who are transferred to a Belgian company or branch that is owned by a foreign company belonging to an international group.
2. Foreigners recruited from outside Belgium either by a Belgian company or subsidiary of a foreign company.
3. Foreign scientists recruited by either a Belgian or foreign scientific establishment in Belgium.

The taxpayer must produce a certificate from his employer indicating the temporary nature of his job and what it is. Though the work is classified as temporary, it can be for an indefinite duration. To qualify the taxpayer must satisfy one of these conditions:
1. His wife and children remain abroad.
2. He continues to maintain a home abroad.
3. The center of his economic interests remains abroad.

A foreign taxpayer on temporary assignment to Belgium may claim a deduction that is designed to cover his additional costs of living abroad. It allows a tax exemption of 30% of his annual salary up to a

69

maximum of B.Fr. 450,000.

Individuals who perform 50% of their business activity outside Belgium are only taxed on remuneration for work performed in Belgium. The total of 240 Belgian work days divided by the number of days spent outside Belgium gives the taxpayer that percentage of his income that will be subject to Belgian tax. Alternatively a flat 50% reduction may be taken. These provisions may also extend to foreign directors of a Belgian enterprise if certain conditions are met.

Foreigners working in Belgium for short periods may be granted a tax exemption by treaty. (The "safe" treaty period specified with the U.S. is 183 days.)

Taxable income is the aggregate amount of net income or profits arising in Belgium from the following sources: income from real estate, income from personal property, income from an occupation or business, and income from miscellaneous sources.

Income from Real Property

Belgian tax law views all real estate as income-producing property. The annual "notional" income, called "net cadastral income" is periodically determined based on the property's annual rental value. This is deducted by B.Fr. 30,000 if the owner occupies his property. If the property is used by the owner for business no extra tax is assessed. If the property is let to others for business, tax is assessed on a figure equal to 200% of the "net cadastral income".

The total real estate advance tax payment (national, provincial and municipal) is a percentage of "cadastral income", of which only 20% is creditable against income tax. None of the advance payment is refunded if it exceeds the tax due.

An additional real estate advance payment is charged to non-resident individuals.

Income from personal property

Personal property income includes dividends, interest (except on tax-exempt securuties), rent, annuity income, and income from capital invested in partnerships. Both Belgian and foreign source income of this type is taxable. Personal property income is included in taxable income at the adjusted gross amount.

For tax purposes, the income of a husband and wife must be combined. There is no provision for separate returns. There is no capital gains tax on individuals.

Tax rates for individuals are progressive. Individuals are entitled to exemptions and allowances. For net taxable income not exceeding B.Fr. 210,000 the tax payable is (depending on number of the taxpayers' dependants) B.Fr. 41,450.

For income above B.Fr. 210,000 the income tax rates are as follows:

Income B.Fr.	Rate
First 210,000—tax payable 41,450	
210,001 to 315,000	30%
315,001 to 415,000	35%
415,001 to 500,000	37.5%
500,001 to 750,000	40%
750,001 to 1,000,000	42.5%
1,000,001 to 2,000,000	47.5%
2,000,001 to 3,000,000	52.5%
3,000,001 to 4,000,000	57.5%
Income in excess of 4 million	60%

A 10% surcharge is levied on income in excess of B.Fr. 500,000. An individual's income tax, before applying the 10% surcharge and other taxes, may not exceed 50% of his taxable income. An additional 6% surcharge may be assessed by the local provinces.

Income tax must be promptly paid within one month after receipt of the return form, or by June 1 of every tax year. 15% penalties are assessed for late filing.

Belgium has no estate taxes. It does have inheritance taxes.

The estates of Belgian residents who are not domiciled in Belgium are subject to tax only on real property located in Belgium (in this case no deductions are permitted).

Registration taxes

Certain events must be registered and a fee paid for the privilege: 2.5% on company formations, 0.2% on leasing of real property, 12.5% on the sale of real property, 1% on mortgages, and 2.5% on issues and increases in a company's share capital.

VAT

The Belgian VAT rates are:

6% (the "reduced rate") for delivery and importation of basic necessities and for the supply of social services.

14% (the "intermediate rate") for delivery and importation of goods of everyday use and for services which are of particular interest from the economic, social or cultural point of view.

18% for goods and services which are not listed elsewhere.

25% (the "surcharged rate") for luxury goods, including automobiles.

VAT returns and payments are due monthly, within 20 days after the end of the calendar month.

Accounting

Corporate reporting standards are comparatively low in Belgium where   71 small family-sized businesses are common. Since there are less than 500 public quoted companies there has been little stimulus for the development of sophisticated accounting systems.

The Commercial Code, contains few provisions relating to company accounts. Generally Belgian company accounts reveal the bare minimum.

Companies are required to prepare an annual set of accounts comprising a balance sheet and income statement. The balance sheet need only show separate totals of fixed assets, current assets, secured and unsecured liabilities. There is no provision for a profit and loss statement and in practice companies rarely disclose their turnover.

The only impetus to the development of accounting standards has come from the tax authorities. The tax laws contain detailed valuation rules which must be followed in the annual accounts.

Depreciation is permitted on both tangible and intangible assets. It is based normally on cost and is written down according to the useful life and potential obsolescence of the equipment. Replacement value cannot be used as a measure for depreciation. The straight line method must be used for depreciation computation. However, the declining balance method may be applied to certain tangible assets if the assets' useful life is between 6 and 19 years. This exception does not apply to buildings, patents, trademarks or goodwill. When the declining balance is used the rate is limited to twice the annual straight line rate or 20% of the assets' value.

Amortization of assets such as patents, trademarks, purchased goodwill and preliminary expenses for company formation are deductible if the taxpayer can prove their actual value is less than their cost.

Depreciation must be recorded to be allowed for tax purposes but in years of low profits or losses it is permissable and common practice to make no charge for depreciation. The position may be ideal for the Belgian businessman but it is disastrous from a commercial or investment viewpoint.

Consolidated accounts are not required. Only one of the top five Belgian corporations consolidates its accounts. Methods of valuation and the effects of any changes in asset values are very rarely disclosed. Fixed assets may be revalued but any surplus may not be distributed and depreciation must be charged on the original value. Inventories are stated at the lower of cost or net realisable value and the LIFO (last in—first out) method is not permitted.

Comparative figures are rarely given. Proposed dividends are not provided for, and long-term leases are seldom capitalised. Intangible assets are stated at cost and goodwill may in certain circumstances be amortised.

72

Losses may be carried forward for five years from the time incurred. An unlimited "carry forward" is permitted for losses which are outside the taxpayer's control. No loss carryback is allowed.

Methods of presentation vary but accounts are certainly not designed for easy reading.

A general shareholders' meeting must approve the continuance of a Belgian company where the accumulated losses exceed 50% of paid up capital.

Business Incentives

There are numerous incentives to industry in Belgium. These include tax relief, land, industrial zones, technical equipment and low interest loans to the value of 75% of fixed assets. (Normally Belgian banks only lend up to 50% of the value of fixed assets.)

Direct capital grants are available in industries where there is high unemployment.

Interest free loans up to 80% of the proposed expenditure are available to help finance research and development for new products and techniques to be used in Belgium. Interest free loans are available to Belgian companies for 50% of expenditures aimed at increasing exports.

Export financing at low rates of interest is also available.

The government may act as a guarantor of long term investment loans in some circumstances or lend money to aid in training personnel in new techniques.

Tax relief available to industry includes exemptions from real estate taxes and capital registration taxes, reduction in capital gains tax upon investment of the capital, accelerated depreciation (straight line or declining balance), loss carry forwards for five years and tax free dividends for five years. Non-Belgian employes of foreign companies, temporarily resident in Belgium, can claim an income tax deduction of 30% of income if they work mainly in Belgium (or 50% if half their time is spent abroad) up to a maximum of $20,000.

Stock Exchange

The main stock exchange is in Brussels. All public issues must be approved by the Commission Bancaire and the Comité de la Cote (Quotation Committee). The Quotation Committe makes sure there is a market for the securities to be offered. Public disclosure of public companies' accounts is a condition of being listed.

Real Estate

Belgium has the most reasonably priced and modern office space in Europe.

Belgians traditionally prefer to rent rather than buy their homes.

There are no restrictions on ownership of land but non-residents may find themselves more susceptible to tax as a result of owning Belgian land.

Labor

No special authorizations are required for persons planning to establish businesses in Belgium. However foreigners require either a work permit or, for self-employed persons and partnerships, a professional card (carte professional). (There are exceptions for some EEC nationals.) Dutch and Luxembourg nationals are considered to be Belgians for these purposes.

Only Belgians can be stockbrokers and travel agents and only Belgian companies can perform public works contracts (there are a few exceptions to these rules).

Work Permits

Work permits are usually issued for one year and are renewable. They are applied for by the employer before the employe goes to Belgium. The application is made to the Ministry of Labor and is accompanied by a medical certificate and two pictures. All Belgian embassies have the necessary forms.

The Foreign Invest Department of the Ministry of Economic Affairs processes the applications of people needed to start new industrial enterprises.

Professional cards are for the self-employed. They are valid for five years and are renewable. U.S. lawyers find them very hard to obtain. EEC residents should find them easy to obtain.

Employees

Belgium has the strictest laws in the Common Market for the protection of its workers. Look before you hire or fire.

There are two classes of employee in Belgium. Workers (blue collar jobs) and employees (white collar work). The difference is important.

Trial periods must be written into employment agreements. For workers they run up to two weeks; for employees no less than one month nor more than three months if the salary is up to B.Fr. 180,000 per annum. If more, a six-month trial period is permitted.

If an employment agreement is not limited in duration in writing it is presumed to be for an indefinite period.

If an employer terminates an agreement without good cause he must pay the wages in full to the end of the contract. This sum may not be more than twice the wages which would have been paid during the legal notice period for a contract of indefinite duration. Termination

74

notices must be in writing.

Employees' contracts must be signed *no later than* the day work begins or else the agreement is presumed to be for an indefinite period.

Contracts for indefinite duration do not have to be in writing. Normally they require 14 days notice for dismissal of an employee and 7 days for a worker.

If employees are dismissed without cause and their annual salary is less than B.Fr. 150,000 they are entitled to three months notice. For each five years of employment there is an additional three months added to the notice period. Employees must generally give half the notice required of the employer. However, the employee never needs to give more than three months notice.

If the annual salary exceeds B.Fr. 150,000 notice cannot be less than three months nor more than four and one-half months. If the employees salary exceeds B.Fr. 300,000 notice cannot exceed six months. For employees in this bracket the notice period is usually fixed by mutual agreements at the time notice is given.

Employment agreements may be cancelled without notice within three days of discovery of grave fault on the part of the employee or worker.

Notice periods for workers begin on Mondays and for employees on the first day of the month.

During the notice period the employee is entitled to time off to look for new work.

Employment agreements may have non-competition clauses good for one year if the employee earns more than B.Fr. 150,000 per annum.

Commercial representatives are considered employees under Belgium law and they are therefore also entitled to notice as well as an indemnity for lost business.

Work weeks are a maximum 45 hours, normally eight hours per day. All categories of labor get overtime pay at a minimum of the standard pay plus 25% for the first two hours and 50% for any balance. Sunday and holiday work calls for 100% overtime pay and a day off during the week.

Belgian social security benefits are extensive and may be carried abroad. Foreigners may be included if their country has a Social Security treaty with Belgium.

Employees and workers are entitled to three weeks vacation per year plus a vacation allowance.

Pregnant women get six weeks leave from work before and eight weeks after birth. Employees under indefinite period arrangements get 30 days sick pay and then social security equal to 60% of their wages.

On closing down a business all people employed one year or more get paid B.Fr. 1,000 for each year of work up to B.Fr. 20,000.

Employers must carry insurance to cover the medical, hospital and disability needs of all personnel as well as death and pension benefits.

Labor unions are not incorporated and are usually affiliated with a political party. The open shop system prevails.

Labor-Management Commissions may be organized at the request of unions, employers or government ministers. They fix working conditions and minimum wages. These *unanimously* approved decisions may then be passed into law by Royal Decree.

Works councils must be set up in all businesses employing at least 50 people. These are labor-management groups which coordinate internal working rules and regulations.

Patents, Trademarks and Copyrights

Patents are valid for 20 years after registration with the office of the Service de la Proprieté Industrielle. Registration is not absolute proof of the validity of the patent as there is no requirement for an examination prior to filing. The application fee is B.Fr. 150 and the annual fees increase on a sliding scale.

Trademarks are valid indefinitely by the first public user. Foreign trademarks should first be registered in their country of origin.

Copyrights are valid for a period of 50 years from the author's death.

V DENMARK

Denmark

KONGERIGET DANMARK

white cross
red background

Total population 5,025,000

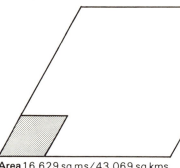

Area 16,629 sq ms/43,069 sq kms

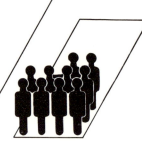

Population density 302 per sq m/116 per sq km

 Form of government Constitutional monarchy. The Monarch exercises executive power through the Council of State headed by the Prime Minister. Legislative power is vested in the Folketing (Parliament) of 179 members including representatives from the Faroe Islands and Greenland. Election to the Folketing is by direct and proportional representation based on equal and universal suffrage.

 Head of state The Monarch/hereditary succession

Voting age 20 years

 Public health Private health insurance
7,134 doctors (1969)
29,485 hospital beds (1969)

 Major imports Raw materials, metals, machinery, fuels, textiles

Major exports Ships, foodstuffs, clothing, pharmaceuticals, furniture, electronics

Copenhagen

```
|0      |50     |100     | 1·50m
|0       |100      |200 km
```

Mercantile marine 3,233
vessels/3,413,855 grt (1970)

Military personnel 41,000

Official language Danish

School-leaving age 16 years

Higher education 16
institutes/47,000 places (1970)

Currency Krone

**Membership of international
organisations** OECD, Council of
Europe, EEC, Nordic Council, the
UN and its agencies

The Great Danes

Introduction

Denmark is a beautiful and thinly populated country inhabited by an industrious people. Like Holland, it is a low country geographically, its highest point a mere 570 feet above seal level. It is the smallest in area of the Nordic Lands (Denmark, Sweden, Finland and Norway).

The Kingdom of Denmark is composed of part of the Jutland Peninsula and some 500 islands (about 100 are inhabited), all of which divides the Baltic and North Seas. There is a common border with Germany in the southeast. The total area is 16,619 square miles, excluding the Faroe Islands (in the North Atlantic, between Scotland and Iceland) and Greenland, which are part of Denmark. The two biggest islands are Fyn (Funen) and Sjaeland (Sealand). Only 7% of the mainland is developed. Nearly 75% of the country is agricultural farmland and 11% woodland and plantations. The rest is heath, peat bogs, swamps, lakes and streams.

Denmark's 5 million people enjoy one of the highest standards of living in the world. Their capital Copenhagen is now the home for close to one-third of all Danes.

Denmark used to be an agricultural nation but rapid technological development has pushed industry to the forefront. Today industrial activity leads in terms of employment, gross national product and export revenue. Situated at the "crossroads" between Scandinavia and Europe, Denmark has naturally always been a seafaring nation. Its communications and transport systems are very good. Much of its industry is concerned with foreign trade. (The U.S. is Denmark's fourth largest trading partner.)

However, the temperate, moist climate, geographical position, largely fertile soil and other factors combine to keep Denmark's land committed mainly to agricultural use. There are few mineral resources, although oil drilling is being undertaken in the Danish sector of the North Sea. Denmark therefore has to manufacture mainly from imported raw materials and to export finished goods and agricultural products. It has suffered a negative balance of payments for years.

80   In addition to their native language, most Danes speak English. The

education system is excellent and English-speaking schools are plentiful.

Denmark is a member of the North Atlantic Treaty Organization (NATO), the United Nations Organization (UNO), the International Monetary Fund, GATT, the OECD and , since January 1, 1973, the Common Market.

Political Structure

Denmark is the oldest kingdom in Europe but has been a constitutional monarchy since 1849. The monarch has no political power. The Parliament (Folketing) consists of one house with 179 members, including two each from the Faroe Islands and Greenland. Members are elected for four years. A vote of "no confidence" can bring down the government. Danish politics are noted for their moderation and high democratic standards.

The commercial and industrial department of the government is the Ministry of Commerce (Handelsministeriet).

Apart from the Faroes (which are self-governing) and Greenland (which is completely integrated with Denmark), the country is divided into 22 countries containing 277 municipalities, including Copenhagen. For other purposes, the country is divided into 72 police districts with the chief constables acting as public prosecutors in the lower courts. They also administer the trading laws and issue trade licenses. Copenhagen has a special status with its own administrative arrangements.

Legal System

The organization and functions of the courts are laid down by the Legislature. Judges are appointed by the monarch on the recommendation of the government. The judges' independence is constitutionally guaranteed.

The highest court in the country is the Supreme Court (Hojestevet) with 15 judges. At least five of these must sit in each case, so that usually the court functions in two divisions. The Supreme Court functions only as a court of appeal.

All cases not falling specifically within the jurisdiction of a lower court are initiated in the High Courts (*Landsvette*). There are two of these: the Eastern High Court (*Ostre Landsvet*) in Copenhagen and the Western High Court (*Vestre Landsvet*) at Viborg.

There are just over 100 lower courts called *Underretter*. Only one judge tries each case. The duties of a judge in the lower court include, besides the actual administration of justice, the functions of bailiff, estate administrator, and notary, together with responsibility for records and registrations.

81

The courts have jurisdiction in all matters not specifically reposed in other authorities by law. All matters, (civil and criminal, administrative and fiscal) come within the sphere of these general courts unless trial by a special court or administrative body is prescribed by legislation. Trial by jury is reserved for the most serious cases.

Denmark has an Ombudsman whose function is to keep an eye on all public officials and agencies to see they perform their duties properly. He has broad powers for investigation and is free of political restraint. Anyone with a complaint against the government can place it before the "Ombridsmand".

General Business Pointers

There is no commercial television in Denmark. The Danes are avid newspaper readers and the circulation for the 67 dailies is about 1.8 million copies.

Denmark is on the metric system.

Vacations

Visits between mid-June and mid-August should be avoided if possible as this is the main vacation period.

New Year's Day
Maundy Thursday
Good Friday
Easter Monday
Store Bededag (Great Prayer Day) (May 18)
Ascension Day
*Constitution Day (June 5)
Whit Monday
*Christmas Eve
Christmas Day
Boxing Day
*New Year's Eve

*Officially public vacations from noon, but many firms and public institutions close for the whole day.

Hours of Business

Banks are open 10:00 to 15:00, Monday to Friday, and in addition 17:00 to 18:00 on Fridays.

Commercial offices are open from 08:00 or 08:30 to 16:30, Monday to Friday. Only retail shops and post offices open on Saturday morning.

Currency and Banking

The currency of Denmark is the kroner (D.Kr.), divided into 100 ore. No foreign banks have been permitted in Denmark. American

Express is the sole exception to this rule. EEC rules will change this.

Denmark has four of the world's 300 largest banks; they are: Copenhagen Handelsbank, Den Dansk Landmandsbank, Privatbanken i Kjobenhaven, and Andelsbanken—Danebank. They provide a full range of banking services under the control of the Central Bank (Danmarks Nationalbank).

Exchange Control

Foreign investment in Denmark is classified as either direct or indirect.

Direct investments are those involving the acquisition of a substantial interest in a Danish business. Permission for such investments must be obtained from the Ministry of Commerce unless the investment is for less than D.Kr. 40,000. Permission is usually granted provided the investment is not in the fields of shipping, agriculture, fishing or arms. Investments in businesses producing alcohol, sugar and yeast are also closely scrutinized.

Permission is not normally granted for indirect investments, (usually) portfolio investments.

International payments must be made through authorized institutions which operate under general license from the Central Bank. Foreign exchange transactions over D.Kr. 2,000 must be reported to the Central Bank.

Firms

1. There are no restrictions on the transfer from Denmark of dividends, profits, interest, royalties or fees of a Danish branch or subsidiary company. Nor are there any restrictions between a Danish branch or subsidiary and its foreign parent company, provided the transactions are made through a bank and, that, in the case of goods, payment is made by the Danish company not earlier than two weeks before nor later than two years after delivery. This period is extended to five years after delivery for ships, aircraft, heavy machinery and plants.

2. Temporary restrictions on exchange control have been introduced under which importers must use the longest terms of credit in a contract.

3. Receipts from most countries must be in convertible currencies but payments to all countries may be in any currency.

4. Foreign parent companies may lend their Danish branches or subsidiaries up to D.Kr. 200,000 per calendar year. They may also grant them credits, within certain limits, to finance purchases abroad. Other foreign borrowings by local companies are strictly controlled by the Central Bank.

5. Proceeds from the sale of investments and the repayment of loans,

83

can be freely transferred abroad.

Individuals

6. Foreigners resident in Denmark are subject to the same exchange control rules as Danes. They must repatriate (to Denmark) liquid assets held abroad unless they obtain a special license from the Central Bank. In most cases they must not export capital without permission from the Central Bank. These rules are administered fairly liberally and money may be transferred without difficulty to your own country to support dependents or as gifts to relatives.

Foreign loans up to D.Kr. 5,000,000 per year may be raised provided they are for at least five years, are drawn in amounts no less than D.Kr. 100,000 and are repaid at no more than 20% per year.

Danish Companies

There are 30,000 small companies in Denmark each with only a handful of shareholders. There are only 300 publicly quoted companies.

Denmark's stock market was not open to foreign companies or issues until it joined the EEC.

The 1973 Companies Act created a new form of smaller company, Anpartsselskaber (APS)—roughly equivalent to a British private company, a German GmbH, or a French SARL—with a minimum equity capital of D.Kr. 30,000. The Act also raised the minimum capital requirements of the only previously existing form of company, Aktieselskab (AS), from D.Kr. 10,000 to D.Kr. 100,000.

Forms of Doing Business

The following are the principal recognized forms of business enterprise in Denmark:

1. Limited liability company (Aktieselskab or A/S).

2. Private company—for smaller business operations (Anpartsselskaber or APS).

3. General partnership (Interessentskab or I.S.)—in which all partners have equal rights and responsibilities.

4. Limited partnerships (Kommanditselskab or K.S.)—in which some partners have full responsibility for partnership obligations while others are limited to the extent of their capital contributions.

5. Limited partnership company (Kommandit-aktieselskab or K.A/S.)—limited partnership where the limited partner is a limited liability company.

6. Partnership with limited liability (Andelsselskab med begrawnset ansvar or Amba).

7. Sole proprietorship (Enkeltmandsfirma)—a one-man business or practice.

8. Cooperative Society (Andelsforening/Brugsforening).

As most foreign investors will use a form of limited liability company or, to a lesser extent, a branch, these forms are considered below in greater detail.

Companies

Formation—to form a limited liability company (A/S), the following procedures are mandatory:

1. A formation agreement must be prepared stating the main objectives of the company and giving all essential data such as company name, share capital and provisions for payment of subscribed shares.

2. The Articles of Association must be drafted in accordance with the formation agreement and contain the standard provisions required by the Companies Act.

3. minimum share capital is D.Kr. 100,000. There must be at least three subscribers. Each must subscribe for at least D.Kr. 500 worth of shares. A Danish company may be a subscriber. The majority of subscribers must be resident in Denmark. If they are not Danish citizens they must have resided in Denmark for five years. A foreign investor organizing a limited liability company may subscribe for all shares except those held by the three persons who qualify under the rules stated above. After registration of the company, two of these qualifying shares may be transferred to nominee shareholders and the third share may be acquired by the foreign investor.

4. A statutory meeting must be held not later than four months after the date of the formation agreement to adopt the Articles of Association and to elect the board of directors and the auditors.

5. Within six months of the date of the formation agreement, the above documents must be supplied to the Registrar of Companies. After approval, the company will be entered in the Register of Companies. There may be considerable delay before formalities are completed. Therefore, it may be expedient to purchase a "ready made" company and alter its constitution to meet your own requirements.

Shares and Shareholders

Shares may be in bearer or registered form (both tranferable), and may be voting or non-voting, preference, or in more than one class. Each class of shares should be created for each company separately according to its needs.

Only par value shares may be issued. There is no minimum par value and each company sets its own minimum. Different classes of shares in the same company may have different par values. Shares may be issued for more than par value but not at a discount. If shares are issued at a premium, the excess funds must be allocated to reserves—

85

unless they are used to cover expenses connected with either the formation of the company or with an increase in share capital. Dividends are usually expressed as a percentage of a share's par value.

The number of shareholders must always be at least three, unless all all or part of the shares are owned by a branch of the Danish government, a Danish limited liability company or a Danish limited partnership company. Thus it is possible for a Danish limited liability company and a foreign corporation to jointly form and be the only two shareholders in a Danish company. In all other cases, if the number of shareholders falls below three for a period of three months, the company is considered wound up. Company officers who are aware of this and continue operations become responsible for fulfilment of company obligations.

A limited liability company may not acquire more than 10% of the par or nominal value of its own share capital for any purpose other than reducing its share capital. These shares must be recorded so as to maintain a record of their par or nominal values. 10% of annual profits must be put into a reserve until it reaches 10% of the share capital. After that only 5% of profits need be set aside until the reserve grows to 25% of the share capital. This reserve can only be used to cover deficits.

There must be a regular annual meeting of shareholders in Denmark. The company's accounts and the agenda for the meeting must be available to shareholders eight days before the meeting.

Rules as to quorums, adjournment of meetings and voting majorities vary and must be stated in the statutes. A general meeting must be called to alter the company's status in any way.

Anpartsselskaber (Private Limited Liability Company)

The main differences between this type of company and an A/S company are:

1. The paid-in share capital need only be D.Kr. 30,000.
2. Less financial disclosure is required.
3. If the company has less than 50 employees and less than D.Kr. 400,000 in capital, it need not have a board of directors.

Company Management

A company is managed by a board of directors of at least three persons (except for small companies). The majority of the directors must reside in Denmark and be either Danish citizens or have been resident in Denmark for five years. If the company name contains a Danish geographical location, or in any way implies a Danish origin, *all* members of the board must reside in Denmark or have been resident in Denmark for five prior years. The Companies Act does not specify where meetings of the board of directors must be held. Directors need not be shareholders.

Large companies (more than 50 employes) must elect two employes to their boards of directors. In addition, the company must contribute to a fund to be used to purchase shares in the company for the employes (up to 50% of the shares).

Branches

If a foreign company establishes a branch in Denmark, it must comply with Danish law in all its Danish activities.

A foreign company may carry on business in Denmark through a registered branch office provided its own country affords similar rights to Danish companies. The name of a registered branch office must include its nationality and show that it is a foreign limited liability company.

Companies which want to open a branch office must complete a Ministry of Commerce registration form. This requests information about the foreign company. An authenticated translation of its incorporation papers and financial statements for the previous three years must also be provided. The registration form and the documents are submitted to the Registrar of Companies and must bear the signatures of all business managers of the branch. A registration fee of D.Kr. 1,500 is payable plus 0.005% of the company's paid-up share capital, up to a maximum fee of D.Kr. 30,000. There are also legal, accountancy and related fees. The registrar must be informed at once of any changes in the Articles of the company.

A branch office must have a manager (or managers). They must have power to bind the company by their signatures. Branch managers must meet the same residence and citizenship requirements as the managers of Danish limited liability companies. The Ministry of Commerce often grants exemptions from this requirement. A branch manager is personally responsible for payment of the company's income tax, customs duties and other liabilities.

The books of a branch office need not be maintained in Denmark; nor need an auditor be appointed. However, it is necessary to prepare audited financial statements for the branch to avoid arbitrary tax assessments.

Accounts

Companies are obliged to maintain high record-keeping standards. Danish accountants are very competent.

In addition to their annual accounts and auditors' report, companies have to publish a directors' report which must include "any information not given in the accounts but important to an evaluation of the company's financial position and results".

Companies must file consolidated accounts for their subsidiaries and associated companies. An "associated company" is one which has a decisive influence on another company's results. Other provisions of Denmark's Companies Act include a suggested layout for accounts and a list of specific profit and loss account disclosure requirements similar to those required in Britain. While Danish companies are allowed to own up to 10% of their own shares, all holdings of a subsidiary company in its parent holding company must be taken into account in computing the 10%.

Depreciation of 30% is allowed in the first year of a capital expenditure.

There are a certain number of peculiarities in the Danish accounting system. Inventories may be undervalued by up to 30%. It is not common to include overheads in valuations. The basis of inventory valuations is rarely disclosed. Purchase commitments (up to 25% of annual purchases) may result in a "write down" of inventories to the extent of 30% of these commitments. The 1973 Companies Act requires all such "write downs" to be disclosed in the accounts.

Partnerships, etc.

No Partnership Act exists in Denmark. Disputes are settled, in the absence of a partnership agreement, by prevailing paractice in the particular trade or profession concerned. The firm's name and the name of the partners may in some cases be entered in the Register of Commerce and published in the Danish State Gazette (Statstidende). Insertion in the Register of Commerce, which is maintained by each municipality, provides protection for the partnership name.

The various partnerships listed at the beginning of this section have in common the principles that general partners have joint and separate liability for obligations of the partnership, and that income tax is imposed on the general or limited partners as individuals and not on the partnership as an entity (except for the Amba). The distinguishing characteristics of the partnerships are:

General partnership—Interessentskab (I.S.)—The name of a general partnership must indicate its nature by the initials I.S. or similar words. An aggrement usually governs the relationships between partners.

Limited partnership—Kommanditselskab (K.S.)—A limited partnership must consist of one or more general partners and one or more limited partners. Partners may be persons or companies, foreign or domestic. A firm's name must include the name of at least one general partner and must indicate that it is a limited partnership by the initials K.S. or by words. The names of limited partners may not appear in the firm name. The firm name, the names of the general

partners, and the amount of liability of the limited partners are
normally stated in the Register of Commerce and published in the
official gazette.

Limited partnership company—Kommandit-aktieselskab—This is a
limited partnership in which a limited liability company is the only
limited partner. None of the general partners may be shareholders in
the limited liability company. The liability of the company is limited
to its share capital. A foreign company cannot be a limited partner in
such a company.

In general, a limited partnership company is subject to the same
regulations as a limited liability company. This form is used infrequently.

Partnership with limited liability—Andelsselskab med begraenset
ansvar (Amba)—This differs from the other partnership forms in that it
is subject to tax as an entity. A person's name may not be used in the
firm name and the initials Amba must be used to show that it is a
limited liability partnership. This form is normally used by
cooperative societies and other entities with at least two limited partners
which want to limit members' liability. Profits are normally distributed
on the basis of capital invested.

Sole proprietorship—Enkeltmandsfirma—A sole proprietorship may
be entered in the Register of Commerce. Registration protects the
business name and indicates its owner. Any name may be selected. The
owner's name may, but need not, appear in the firm name.

Cooperative society—Andelsforening/Brugsforening—These societies
are more common in Scandinavia than in Europe. There is no special
statute for cooperative societies and formation is easy. Members'
liability may be limited or unlimited, depending on the Articles of
Association. It is normally limited, in which case the initials m.b.a.
must appear in its name.

A cooperative society is subject to minimal taxation. Individual
members are not taxed. Profits of cooperative societies are normally
distributed on the bais of turnover or volume of business done with
each member of the society.

Tax in Denmark
General

Consumer taxes and customs duties make up roughly 50% of
Denmark's total tax revenue. Customs duties, which at the beginning of
the century were a source of considerable revenue, now have scarcely
any fiscal significance.

One of the main characteristics of consumer taxation in Denmark is
that it is based on taxing only a rather small number of commodity
groups. The most important taxable items are tobacco, beverages, and
motor vehicles. The tax was imposed in 1967 by the introduction of

89

value-added tax (VAT). The VAT rate is 15%.

Individuals

Foreigners staying in Denmark for less than three years get a special tax allowance of D.Kr. 8,000 plus 25% of their gross salary each year. Normally exemptions are D.Kr. 5,400 plus 20% of earned income and D.Kr. 720 for each child. Non-residents pay tax only on income earned in Denmark.

Personal income tax is levied both by the central and local governments. The rates of central government taxes are the same throughout the country. Local government income taxes average about 40% of all income tax and vary between local governments. Both central and local government taxes are progressive, the central government tax being considerably higher.

The highest rate of combined central and local government tax is normally 60%-65%. The maximum may not exceed 66.66%, regardless of the amount of local government tax. The maximum rates usually apply to that part of the income which exceeds D.Kr. 80,000 (about $13,000). In addition to these taxes, individuals must make social security contributions and most pay a church tax as well. Individuals must also pay a wealth tax on their net capital assets every year.

Capital gains are not normally included in calculating personal income tax. There is, however, a special tax at 30% on certain capital gains accruing from the sale of real estate and shares.

The tax year runs from April 1 to March 31.

Companies

Tax for Danish companies is charged at the rate of 36% on yearly earnings. As in the U.S., the tax is imposed on total net earnings whether paid out in dividends or transferred to asset or reserve accounts. There is a special deductible allowance which amounts to 50% of taxable income or 2.5% of the issued and fully paid share capital, whichever is lower. Consequently, the effective rate is 18% up to the level of 5% of the paid share capital. Income on foreign business operations is taxed at half the standard rate and is therefore effectively between 9% and 18%. This is a great encouragement to the export trade. The central government takes 85% of the revenue from company taxes. Local governments take the rest.

Branches of foreign companies pay a flat 34% of net income (without a special deduction allowance). "Headquarters" companies and sales offices which cannot "close" deals themselves are free of tax.

Dividends are subject to a 30% withholding tax. The tax treaty between Denmark and the U.S. reduces this to 15% (or 5% when the company is owned 95% or more by U.S. interests).

Gifts above a minimum amount are taxed as "special income". A 50% tax is imposed on "special income" received by companies and individuals (such as the sale of stock warrants).

An annual tax, which averages about 3%, but which varies considerably between local governments, is charged on land, based on quadrennial valuations.

Foreign Investment in Denmark

Although no preferential encouragement is given to foreign enterprises to set up business in Denmark, the government believes in full competition. Foreign companies are treated in the same manner as Danish companies subject to certain exchange control regulations.

However, owners of farms are required to live on them and to derive their income mainly from farming (with some exceptions). This discourages foreigners from owning farms.

Rules applicable to all Businesses

1. *Before commencement*—A license must be obtained before any trading activities are begun, whether by a company, a branch, a partnership or an individual. In Copenhagen, this is issued by the municipal authorities and elsewhere by the police. A separate license is required for each municipality in which the business has a permanent establishment. The cost of a license is D.Kr. 80. There are further requirements for specialized activities. Generally professional firms do not need a license. In partnerships, each partner should have a license.

Individuals who apply for a license must normally be Danish, over 20, resident in the country and legally free to manage their own affairs. Foreigners, however, are eligible if they fulfil the other conditions and have a passport with residence and labor permits stamped in it.

Registers of Commerce, giving particulars of most industrial and commercial businesses, are kept in Copenhagen and in each provincial town. The exceptions are one-man enterprises where registration is optional, and limited companies which are listed in the Company Register in Copenhagen. Registration must be made before trading begins. The details to be disclosed include the identity of the owner(s) or manager(s); the arrangements for entering into contracts or other commitments; and the names of those authorized to sign on behalf of the business.

2. *After formation*—The status of a foreign-owned company is equal to that of a Danish-owned company. Foreign-owned companies can operate freely almost anywhere in Denmark, can engage in any legitimate trade, buy or rent premises and hire managers and other staff.

Everyone doing business in Denmark on a regular basis must be listed on the Trade Register. Companies must include their

91

registration number on their letterheads and order forms.

Tax Investment Incentives

No special tax incentives are offered to attract foreign investment. However, foreign entities may utilize any of the incentives offered to Danish businesses. (See section on taxes for special treatment of branches, headquarters companies, and exporters). Generous depreciation, amortization and writing-down allowances are combined with a comparatively low rate of corporation tax to encourage new investments whether made by foreign or by Danish businesses.

Business Incentives

1. State aid and development areas—Businesses wishing to set up in certain areas designated by the 1972 Regional Development Act may obtain financial assistance from the Danish government. The areas covered by the Act are North, West and South Jutland and the group of islands south of Sealand. All of these, except West Jutland, are also eligible for special investment grants.

In approved cases, the government will guarantee bank loans for up to 90% of the initial cost of the required capital investment against reasonable security. These loans bear interest at $7\frac{1}{4}\%$ and are repayable in 20 years. Advances may also be made for purposes of relocation, extension, rationalization of labor and for conversion of production. In certain cases, the government itself may make the loan.

Labor

Anyone staying in Denmark longer than three months requires a residence permit. These are freely given as are work permits for foreign managerial and technical staff. But work permits for ordinary employment are hard to obtain. Work permits are issued by the police.

Danish workers are highly skilled. All Danish businesses must make social security contributions for their employees, (about 15% of wages), as well as health, accident and disability insurance. Employees are entitled to a miniumum of four weeks paid vacation each year.

There is no minimum wage or maximum work week legislation. Hourly workers may be discharged without notice or severence pay. Regular salaried staff are entitled to 1-6 months notice.

Unions are organized on a trade basis rather than an industry basis.

Real Estate

While no permission is required to rent space, ownership of real estate by a foreigner requires official approval. This is normally given, by the Ministry of Justice, if the property is to be used for industrial or commercial purposes.

Patents, Trademarks and Copyrights

Foreign companies intending to export goods to Denmark are officially advised to patent their products and register their trademarks in that country.

The Danish Patent Act provides non-renewable protection for 17 years but "patents of addition" are protected only for the unexpired life of the main patent. In case of the withdrawal or invalidation of the main patent, the "patent of addition" remains in force for the unexpired life of the original patent.

The patent applicant must be the inventor or his legal successor. A foreigner who applies for a patent must appoint a Danish agent. The invention should be in use within three years of the patent being issued or compulsory licensing may be required. An application fee of D.Kr. 400 is charged in addition to minor annual fees if the patent is accepted.

Exclusive trademarks are given to the first applicant for a period of 10 years. They are renewable for another 10 years, within the period between one month prior to expiration and six months after that.

Copyright protection is for the author's life plus 50 years, and covers all forms of literary and musical works.

Stock Market

The stock market in Denmark is small and was closed to foreign companies until 1973 when Denmark joined the Common Market. It is not a significant factor in Danish business.

General Information

Those seeking further information about Denmark should consult the following information sources.

1. Udenrigsministeriets Handelsafdeling (Foreign Ministry Trade Relations Department)
   Amaliegade 18
   DK-1256 Copenhagen K
   Telephone: (01) 12 30 60

2. Tourism:
   a. Danmarks Turistraad (Danish Tourist Board)
      Vesterbrogade 6D
      DK-1620 Copenhagen V
      Telephone: (01) 11 14 15

3. Commerce
   For general information, contact:
   Grosserer-Societetet,

93

Danmarks Engros Handelskammer (Copenhagen Chamber of
Commerce)
BØrsen
DK-1217 Copenhagen K
Telephone: (01) 15 53 20

This organization is the main and official representative of the
Danish wholesale and import trade. Its foreign-trade department can
supply information on the export activities of member companies,
including export merchants.

4. Industry
   a. Industriraadet (Federation of Danish Industries)
      H.C. Andersens Boulevard 18
      DK-1596 Copenhagen 5
      Telephone: (01) 15 22 33

   b. Landsforeningen Dansk Arbejde (National Association for the
      Promotion of Danish Enterprise)
      KØbmagergade 22
      DK-1150 Copenhagen K
      Telephone: (01) 14 40 28

The extensive files maintained by this organization can help locate
the manufacturer of virtually any Danish product.

VI FRANCE

France

REPUBLIQUE FRANCAISE

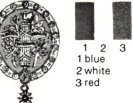

1 2 3
1 blue
2 white
3 red

Total population 51,487,400

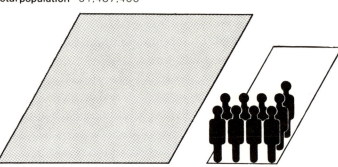

Area 212,919 sq ms/551,601 sq kms

Population density 242 per sq m/93 per sq km

Form of government Presidential democracy. Executive power is vested in the President and the Government headed by a Prime Minister. Legislative power is exercised by the National Assembly of 490 members and the Senate of 283 deputies. Election to the National Assembly is by direct, proportional, and universal suffrage. Election to the Senate is for 9 years by members of the National Assembly and representatives of the Municipal and General Councils of the Departments.

Head of state The President/elect for 7 years by direct referendum

Voting age 21 years

Public health Private health insurance and contributory state health insurance
67,830 doctors (1970)
662,189 hospital beds (1970)

Major imports Raw materials, machinery, fuels, chemicals, minerals

Major exports Chemical products aircraft, textiles, motor vehicles, foodstuffs, drink

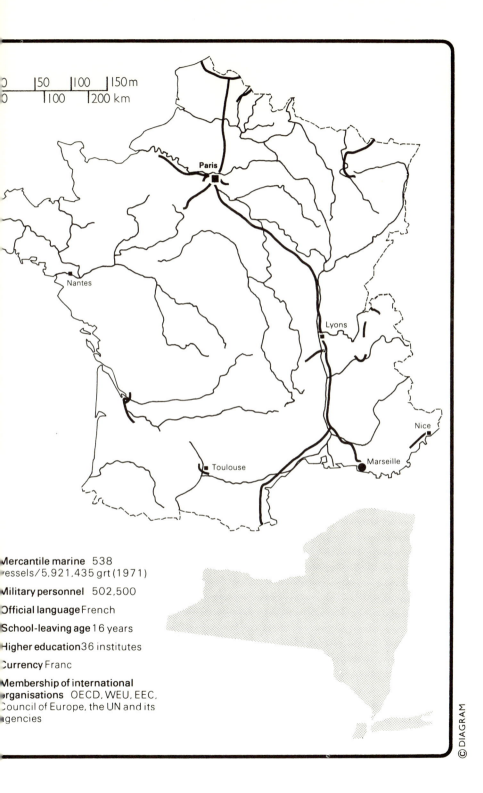

Mercantile marine 538
vessels/5,921,435 grt (1971)

Military personnel 502,500

Official language French

School-leaving age 16 years

Higher education 36 institutes

Currency Franc

Membership of international
organisations OECD, WEU, EEC,
Council of Europe, the UN and its
agencies

© DIAGRAM

Vive la Difference

Introduction

France (including Corsica) is the largest country in Western Europe encompassing 213,000 square miles. It is a beautiful land containing every geographical feature from the rough North Atlantic coast of Brittany, to the magnificent French Alps and the shimmering Cote D'Azur on the Mediterranean Sea. Together with a temperate climate and fertile soil, its population of 52 million (one-third under 21) have combined to create a nation renowned for its beauty, culture and wine.

France touches every other Common Market state on the Continent except Denmark. Monaco on the south coast has a special relationship with France.

France has had the fastest rate of growth within the Common Market. The French are determined to maintain it.

Paris, its capital, is one of the most beautiful cities in the world, it is also becoming one of the most congested. Its population is over 9 million. France is developing a regional policy to encourage business to move away from Paris.

France, a founder member of the EEC, pursues an independent line. It left NATO, discouraged Americn investment and froze Britain out of the EEC for 10 years.

Although much of French industry is government owned (and despite the size of the Communist party), it is essentially a free economy where the government acts as "big brother" to business.

Although the farm population has been decreasing, agriculture is still an industry of major importance. Approximately 14% of the active population is engaged on the land. Wheat is the most important single crop. Fruit, vegetables and wine are also produced in quantities permitting substantial exports. France is self-sufficient in dairy products.

The problem of matching agricultural output to demand, not just in France, but throughout the Common Market is one of perennial difficulty.

Today, a more powerful France is changing its policies. Britain is a member of the Common Market and the U.S., its fourth largest trading partner, is a major investor in France.

By way of example, in France's Western Development Region, 51 out of 89 new industries started in 1973, were American owned.

France uses the metric system.

The French are very particular about their language and speak it correctly. They generally prefer not to speak English but for business they may bend a little. There are a number of English speaking schools.

Communications are excellent. Marseilles and Le Havre are the fourth and fifth largest European ports. Le Havre aims to become No. 2 by 1975.

Newspapers, TV and advertising are among the best in Europe.

Political Structure

France is a republic, ruled under a Constitution adopted in 1958 by popular referendum. The Constitution provides for separate executive, legislative and judicial powers. The chief executive is the President, elected for a seven-year term. He appoints the Prime Minister and the members of the cabinet. The French Parliament consists of two houses: the National Assembly with 487 deputies, elected for five-year terms by popular vote; and the Senate with 247 members, appointed for nine-year terms by an electoral college. The Prime Minister and his cabinet *may not* be members of the National Assembly. (If they are, they must resign their seats on accepting cabinet office.) The Assembly must approve all presidential appointments *en bloc*.

For administrative purposes, metropolitan France (including Corsica) is divided into 95 departments which are governed by "Prefects" (appointed by the President and responsible to the Ministry of the Interior) and "General Councils" (elected). The departments are grouped into 22 regions. Four departments exist outside continental France—Guiana, Guadeloupe and Martinique in the Caribbean, and Reunion in the Indian Ocean. The Republic also includes the Pacific Ocean territories of New Caledonia, New Hebrides and French Polynesia, which are self-governing.

Legal System

The law guarantees the freedom of all citizens, and the judiciary was created with this objective. The civil courts handle disputes between individuals. They consist of lower courts (which deal with minor cases), superior courts, a Court of Appeal, and the Supreme Court of Appeal (Cour de Cassation) which is the highest judicial authority. Tribunals handle commercial law cases and arbitration boards decide disputes between employers and employes. There are also administrative courts with right of appeal to the Council of State (*Conseil d'Etat*) which consider disputes between government administrative

99

branches and individuals.

The commercial and economic department of the government is the Ministry of Economics and Finance.

Currency and Banking

The currency of France is the franc (F.Fr.).

The French banking industry is strong. It offers a full range of services. The Banque National de Paris is the fifth largest in the world after the Bank of America, First National City Bank, Chase Manhattan and Barclays Bank. Three of the largest banks in France are government owned (as is much of French industry). One of these is the Banque de France which deals with foreign exchange matters. Banking is under the control of the Commission de Controle des Banques.

Paris is competing with London to become the banking capital of the Common Market. Most major U.S. banks have offices in Paris.

Business Hours and Vacations

Banking hours are 09:00—16:00, Monday through Friday; government offices have a staggered nine-hour day from 08:30 to 18:00, Monday through Friday with two hours for lunch.

Shops (local) are open 08:30 to 12:00 and 14:00 to 19:30, Tuesday through Saturday.

Shops (fashionable) are open 09:00 to 12:00 and 14:00 to 18:00 Tuesday through Saturday.

Department store hours are 09:30—19:30 Tuesday through Saturday (some are open on Monday).

Banks close a half day before public vacations.

The French usually extend their vacations to have long weekends wherever possible. Vacations are as follows:

New Year's Day
Easter Monday
Labor Day
Ascension Day
Whit Monday
Bastille Day (July 14)
Assumption
All Saints Day
Armistice Day (November 11)
Christmas Day
Boxing Day (Alsace-Lorraine District only)

Exchange Control

French exchange control rules are subject to rapid changes to meet new situations.

There are at times two rates of exchange. There is the official (or "commercial") franc which is supported by the Bank of France and is used for the payment of goods and service. The other is the "financial" franc for transfers of capital, salaries, interest, dividends and for tourism.

Foreigners wishing to set up or buy a company in France must get the consent of the Ministère de L'Economic et des Finances. Decisions are influenced by the potential benefit to the French economy and how much of the company will be owned by foreigners (its hard to get past 50-50).

Foreign loans under F.Fr. 2,000,000 need no approval; but larger loans do. Purchases of houses and French shares (up to 20% of a company's capital require no approval.

Repatriation of an investment and its profits is freely given but certain reporting requirements exist.

Imports

For imports involving more than F.Fr. 10,000, there is an elaborate exchange control procedure. If payment is by documentary credit (or certain other methods), currency can be obtained up to 30 days before the goods are due to be shipped from the exporting country; otherwise currency can be obtained only after the goods are cleared by customs and not more than 30 days before payment is due under the contract.

This does not apply to imported goods valued from F.Fr. 250 to 10,000; But payment cannot be made until after the goods have arrived (except under certain conditions, e.g. when payment is by documentary credit, or remission of documents, or presentation of transport documents).

For imports worth less than F.Fr. 250, it is only necessary for the importer to show to an approved bank or post office an invoice or letter from the foreign supplier in order to arrange payment.

When payment has to be made before importation the importer must produce the commercial contract as evidence. If the goods have already been imported into France, documentary evidence of their passage through French customs will be required. Similarly transfers of currency out of the country or credits to foreign accounts in payment for imports have to be proved by documentary evidence.

Regulations on foreign-owned Businesses

1. *Before formation*—A foreign company wanting to establish a sunsidiary or branch in France or to purchase an existing French company must apply for Ministry of Finance permission, giving full particulars of the intended operation. If the foreign company wants to increase its existing control of a French undertaking, it must also seek

101

permission. The same applies if its French subsidiary wishes to make an acquisition.

Within two months of the application being filed, the Ministry may either postpone the proposed transactions or give the go-ahead. Each application is accepted or rejected on its merits. As a practical matter it is good business to have French partners to the extent of at least 50% of any French compnay.

The approval of the Ministry of Finance is necessary before the shares of a foreign-owned company can be quoted on the Stock Exchange. Exceptions are operations connected with loans guaranteed by the French government and shares which rank with or may be substituted for already quoted shares.

2. *After formation*—A forien-owned company in France has the same status as a French-owned company, and foreign nationals working in France have the same rights and responsibilities as French citizens.

Direct investment in France by foreign companies must be substantially financed by a foreign currency but the government does not insist on French participation either in capital or management. There are no restrictions on foreign companies operating in particular places or industries or on owning land or property. However, there are certain "disincentives" in the Paris area. The employment of foreign managers, engineers and other staff is permitted as long as the entry conditions are observed. However, as a practical matter, you must do things the French way or you will not be permitted to do them at all.

France is a signatory to the 1965 "Convention on the Settlement of Investment Disputes", under which an international center for arbitration and conciliation was set up as a department of the World Bank. The center is available to resolve differences concerning investment projects, where one party is a government or government agency and the other a foreign national.

Forms of Business

Foreign investors may adopt any form of business recognized in France. The principal ones are:

1. Companies (*Sociétés de capitaux*)

   a. Société Anonyme (S.A.) is a public or private limited liability company. "Public" means quoted on a stock exchange or otherwise offered or advertised to the public at large.

   b. Société à résponsabilité limitée (S.A.R.L.) is a limited liability company with certain partnership features.

2. Partnerships (*Sociétés de Personnes*)

   a. Société en nom collectif (S.N.C.) is a general partnership in which all the partners are jointly and separately liable for the debts of the partnership.

b. Société en commandité is a mixed partnership made up of one or more general partners and limited partners whose liability is limited to their investment and who cannot take part in management.

Partners are taxed individually and not as a partnership.

Another business form is being used increasingly by groups of companies wishing to cooperate, but not to merge and so lose their individual independence. This is a joint venture known as a "groupement d'intérêt économique" (G.I.E.), and it is formed by registering the contract between the companies concerned at the Registre du Commerce. There is a minimum of legal requirements and the contract itself sets out the rules to be followed. This form of association may be used as a model for "cross-frontier" ventures by the EEC in the future.

Managers of partnerships are called "gerants". Partners are not eligible for all social security benefits available to employees.

S.A. Companies

This is the form of organization usually established by foreign investors. The statutory authority is the 1966 Companies Act. A company's life is not perpetual in France as it is in the U.S. Every company has a statutory life of 99 years but the term is renewable.

How to form a company

A declaration of subscription (declaration de souscription et de versements) must be filed with a notary and articles of incorporation (statuts) in French must be prepared defining the capital and constitution of the company. Before the company acquires legal status, these documents must be lodged with the Companies Registry (Registre du Commerce) and the appropriate registration fee paid. After that, the shareholders, of whom there must be at least seven for an S.A. company, hold their first meeting to appoint the necessary officials.

The minimum authorized share capital for a public company is F.Fr. 500,000, and for a private S.A. company F.Fr. 100,000. The capital must be fully subscribed in cash or other assets. If subscription is by cash, 25% of the nominal value of each share must be paid initially, and the balance within five years of the company's incorporation. Shares issued for assets other than cash (*apparte en nature*) must be wholly paid for on issue. The value of those assets must be certified by a commissioner for contributions (*commissaire aux apparti*). Such shares cannot be transferred for at least two years.

Cost of Formation

1. Registration duty of 1% on cash contributions and 11.4% on

103

certain asset contributions (property and intangibles—such as goodwill).

2. Notary's fees are related to capital of the company on an increasing scale. For example: capital up to F.Fr. 200,000: fee F.Fr. 875; capital up to F.Fr. 500,000: fee F.Fr. 475; capital up to F.Fr. 1,000,000: fee F.Fr. 1,975.

3. Legal publication and tax stamps: F.Fr. 1,500—2,000.

4. Fees for the services of professional advisers are on average higher than in the U.S.

Shares and Shareholders

There are no restrictions on the maximum number, nationality or residence of shareholders, who may be individuals or companies.

Shares (actions) with differing rights may be issued. All must have a minimum nominal value of F.Fr. 100 each and cannot be issued at less than par. They may be in bearer form (except for shares given to executives, shares issued for assets for the first two years of the company's existence, and shares not fully paid). There are no limitations on the transfer of shares. No transfer certificate is required and there is no transfer tax. Bearer shares are transferred by delivery. Companies which have been in existence for at least two years and have had two balance sheets approved by shareholders may issue debentures (provided that the nominal capital is fully paid).

Management

1. *Management and Supervision*—A company may be managed by either a president and board of directors (administrateurs); or a shareholders' council (conseil de surveillance) and a management committee (directoire).

A board of directors, numbering from 3 to 12, is elected by the shareholders, If named in the Articles of Incorporation, they serve for three years but if appointed at a shareholders' meeting the term is six years. A company can be a director if it nominates a specific person to represent it on the board. Directors must each hold at least one qualifying share. The remaining directors may replace a director who dies or resigns (the appointment must subsequently be approved by the shareholders). In a general meeting, shareholders may dismiss a director at any time. Foreigners can be directors of French companies. So can employees with two years service. Not more than one-third of the directors can be company employees. No one may be a director of more than eight companies. The presence of at least half the directors is needed for a quorum but a director may act as proxy for one other director (the appointment being by letter or telex). Board meetings need not be held in France. Directors are paid attendance fees (*jetons de présence*) and may receive a share of the profits (*tantièmes*) which must be related to the amounts paid as dividends. They may also have employment contracts for special responsibilities. The powers and duties of directors include the election of the president (*directeur général*) and managers, the making of decisions affecting the management of the company, the preparation of the annual financial accounts and the calling of shareholders' meetings.

The president's term of office is renewable but he may not be president of more than two companies at once. The board may appoint a general manager (*gérant*), (two, if the capital exceeds F.Fr. 500,000) to assist the president. The general manager need not be a director or a shareholder.

The company is responsible to third parties even if its executives are found to have acted improperly.

Following a trend in Europe, an alternative "two-tier" form of management—a shareholders' council (*conseil de surveillance*) controlling a management committee (*directoire*)—was introduced in 1966. Its purpose is to separate the functions of control and management.

The shareholders. council consists of 3 to 12 members whose terms of office are broadly similar to those of directos. The council appoints the management committee (two to five members) for renewable terms of four years. Companies with a nominal capital of less than F.Fr. 250,000 may have only one manager. No person can be simultaneously on both the shareholders' council and the management committees of more than two companies at the same time.

A management committee is responsible for the running of the company. Its members salaries are fixed by the shareholders' council. Members of the management committe may be salaried employes of the company, and members do not have to be shareholders. They may be dismissed only by the shareholders on the advice of the shareholders' council. Non-residents may be appointed to the committee.

If a company has more than 50 employes, a works committee (*comité d'entreprise*) must be appointed. This committee may send two representatives to board or shareholders' council meetings; not, however, of the management committee. The two representatives have no voting rights at these meetings.

2. *The Shareholders in General Meeting*—Within six months of the end of every financial year a meeting of shareholders must be held to adopt the annual audited accounts; to receive reports by the management on the year's activities; to discharge the board members from their responsibilities for the year; to allocate profits; and to conduct any other relevant business. A quarter of the shareholders must be represented. A shareholder's spouse or another shareholder is

the only person eligible to act as a proxy at these meetings.

Reserves, Distributions and Losses

The first 5% of annual profits must be transferred to reserves until the reserves total 10% of the authorized capital. After that, profits are allocated for payment of a first dividend (often 5%); and then a "super-dividend" (*tantième*) and to reserves. Normally all profits each year are distributed in one form or another.

If accumulated losses exceed 75% of the authorized capital, an extraordinary general meeting of stockholders must be called to determine whether or not the company should be put into liquidation. The decision must be published and filed with the Registre du Commerce. If the company decides to continue, the situation must be corrected within two years either by earning profits or issuing fresh capital. If at the end of the two-year period, the accumulated losses are still above the 75% figure the company must either reduce its capital proportionately or go into liquidation.

S.A.R.L. Companies

Although similar rules apply to S.A.R.L.'s and S.A.'s, there are a number of important differences. The range of membership of an S.A.R.L. is from 2 to 50. It may not engage in banking, insurance, air transport and a number of other activities. The minimum capital is F.Fr. 20,000, all of which must be paid up on incorporation. The services of a notary are not required except when shares are paid for with property. Shares are not issued and interest (parts sociales) in the S.A.R.L. are transferred by notarial deed which carries a 4.8% transfer tax. There are restrictions on transfers. There are wider powers for the appointment of proxies than in an S.A.

Approval of amendments to the Articles of Incorporation requires a 75% majority of the shareholders. The admission of new members requires a majority vote of shareholders representing a majority of the company's capital. After two years, a 75% majority vote may approve a change to the S.A. company form. Since the formation of an S.A.R.L. is often quicker and cheaper than that of an S.A., and since there are no tax consequences in the change, some companies setting up in France initially form an S.A.R.L.

An S.A.R.L. is run by one or more managers (*gérants*) who need not be members of the company. Their powers, responsibilities and methods of payments are broadly in line with those applicable to directors or members of a management committee, but there is no limit to the share of profits which may be allocated to them. A gérant may be a foreigner and he may be removed from office by holders of more than 50% of the company's capital.

An S.A.R.L. is not allowed to issue negotiable bonds or raise capital from the public.

Branches

In order to form a branch, a foreign company must prove its existence by producing an official translation and a certified copy of its charter, by-laws, and other relevant documents, together with a "certificat de coutume" (a legal document which states that it has not broken the laws of its home country).

The name of the company must be entered in the Registre du Commerce and declared to the tax authorities. Under French law, a foreign company that sets up a branch is directly liable for all debts of the branch. A branch is managed by a "directeur", who must be resident in France.

A branch is considered a permanent establishment, and under French tax law is treated in almost the same way as other companies.

French Tax System

All French taxes are levied by the national government.

The bulk of French tax receipts comes from turnover taxes, principally the taxe sur la valeur ajoutée (value-added tax). The rest comes from income, profits, payroll, municipal and registration taxes.

Company Income Tax

Company income tax (*impôt sur le bénéfice des sociétés*) is paid on net income at a flat rate of 50%. French and foreign companies are generally taxable only on income from French sources. All overhead expenses, including payroll, social security charges, rent and the like are deductible. Other deductions are taxes, charitable contributions, interest, depreciation, the creation of certain foreign establishments, exceptional research expenses, exceptional items relating to operations which are in line with the government's territorial development policy and reserves.

A new law aims to improve the lot of small businesses in France by more equitable, progressive. less complicated taxation and improvements in the old-age pension system. The law will also curb the spread of large supermarkets and clamp down on "discriminatory" practices, such as distortive price calculations and misleading advertising.

Personal Income Tax

Individuals pay a progressive tax on personal income of all types (*impôt sur le revenu des personnes physiques*). The maximum rate is 60% on incomes of F.Fr. 92,125 (about $20,000). The aim of recent tax legislation has been to share wealth more evenly. All persons

107

domiciled in France are, in principle, taxable on their world-wide
income from all sources. Overseas income of persons not domiciled in
France is exempt if they can show that this income is taxed in their
country of origin. French residents not domiciled in France, are taxed
either on their income from French sources or on the basis of five times
the rental value of their residence(s) in France, whichever is higher.

Individuals are not subject to capital gains tax from the sale of
non-business assets except: the sale of real property (held for less than
10 years), the sale of shares, and gains on liquidation of a company
(15%). Taxable income is the total of the net income or loss from each
category of income, subject to various deductions.

Value-Added Tax

The bulk of French tax receipts (around 58%) is derived from
turnover and sales taxes, of which the most substantial is the
value-added tax (*taxe sur la valeur ajoutée*) or TVA. VAT rates are
graduated according to how necessary the products are. The highest,
33.3% is on luxury goods. The standard rate is 23%. Other rates are
$7\frac{1}{2}$% and 17.6%.

Taxes on Dividends, Interest and Royalties

1. *Dividends*—There is a 25% withholding tax on dividends paid to
non-resident (individuals or companies). Dividends paid to residents of
France (individuals or companies) are not subject to withholding tax,
and are entitled to a tax credit (*avoir fiscal*) equal to 50% of the
dividend received.

The profits of a French branch of a foreign company are subject to
the 25% withholding tax.

2. *Interest*—Interest from French sources paid to non-residents
(individuals or companies) is usually subject to a 25% withholding tax.
These interest payments are usually not deductible. Residents can
pay the 25% withholding tax to cover all French tax obligations.
This rate will go up to $33\frac{1}{3}$% (subject to certain conditions). The
withholding tax on bank deposits and bonds is either nil or 10%.
Residents, receive a F.Fr. 1,000 allowance for interest income.

Royalties

Royalties paid to non-resident individuals or companies for the use of
patents, trademarks, copyrights or "know-how" carry a 24%
withholding tax. The rate applies to the amount of the royalties less a
standard allowance of 20%. Therefore, the effective withholding tax is
reduced to 19.2%.

Refunds for U.S. Owners of French Stock

The U.S.-France income tax treaty can allow non-resident U.S. stockholders a refund in excess of the French withholding tax. This is done by means of a U.S. tax credit for French withholding tax and a rebate from France to non-residents. The I.R.S. ruling "Revenue Procedure 73-24, I.R.B. 1973-64 21" shows how stockholders can obtain this refund.

French corporate tax follows the "imputation" system. The stockholder in a French corporation is considered to have paid half the corporate tax, which is imposed at a 50% rate. The stockholder reports the dividend he receives,plus a "gross up" of 50% of that amount, and is allowed a credit against his French tax for that 50%.

Under the U.S.-French income tax treaty, a tax of 15% is withheld in France on French dividends paid to U.S. residents. But a protocol to the treaty extends imputation benefits to the U.S. stockholder. A U.S. stockholder is entitled to a refund from the French tax authorities, with respect to French corporate tax. The amount refunded is more than the 15% withheld in France. The gross dividend and the gross refund are both considered dividends for U.S. tax purposes, and credit is allowed for French tax paid.

The refund of French tax is obtained by filing the original and two copies of French Form R.F.-1A.E.U. (No. 5052), Application for Refund, available from the Office of International Operations, Internal Revenue Service, P.O. Box 19007, Washington D.C. 20036, Attention: CP 10:2.

For stocks represented by American Depository Receipts (A.D.R.'s) special procedures apply.

Transfer Taxes

Registration or recording taxes are charged on the sale of certain assets, including the following: real estate, shares, goodwill, leasehold rights, and the computation of transfer taxes.

Inheritance Taxes

Inheritance taxes are practically the only tax on capital applicable in France. For non-residents they apply only to assets which are situated in France.

Local Taxes

The following taxes are levied by the state for local government: rates, real estate tax (contribution forciere), residence tax (contribution mobiliere), and business licence tax (patente).

Capital Gains and Losses

Taxes on capital gains and losses vary according to whether the gains or losses are short- or long-term.

The short-term gains and short-term losses are set off against each other. If there is a net short-term gain, it is taxed at the ordinary rate of company tax of 50%. However, this gain may be spread equally over the present and the two succeeding fiscal years (except in the case of sale of an entire business).

If there is a net short-term loss, the loss is deducted from the net operating profits of that fiscal year. If the net operating profits are insufficient to absorb all the loss, it can be carried forward for up to five years.

Long-term gains and losses are also set off against each other. If there is a net long-term gain, it may be set off against the net operating loss for the year or those losses carried forward from preceding years. It may also be set off against net long-term losses carried forward from the 10 preceding years. The balance of the net long-term gain is taxed at a reduced rate of 10%. The remaining 90% is carried on the books as a special reserve. When dividends are paid it is added to the taxable profit on which company tax is paid, after deducting $-\frac{1}{9}$ of the amount distributed.

If there is a net long-term loss, it can be set off against long-term gains (but not against net operting profits or short-term gains) during the next 10 fiscal years.

Accounts

All French companies must comply with the rules set up by the "Le Plan Comptable" (accounting law). It establishes the requirements for company accounts. However, there is no enforcement body for "Le Plan" aside from the tax authorities.

Provision must be made for depreciation and liabilities. Assets must be valued at cost or market value—whichever is lower.

Details of holdings representing more than 10% of the voting power of a company must be reported as well as transactions with companies under common directorships. Expenses of top executives are closely scrutinized.

Depreciation in France is pretty straightforward. Both the "straight line" and declining balance systems are used. In the case of buildings for scientific purposes accelerated depreciation is allowed.

French accounting standards are poor.

Investment Incentives
State Aid for New Industries

110   There are many incentives to encourage industry to disperse more

evenly throughout the country. The efforts of the various government departments are coordinated by the Délégation à L'Aménagement du Territoire et à L'Action Régionale (DATAR), in Paris. DATAR is always willing to advise foreign investors on the range of available benefits. Benefits must be applied for before the investment is made.

The incentives include cash grants (usually up to 25% of the value of the investment), contributions towards the cost of moving plant to other areas, tax relief (including accelerated depreciation allowances) and subsidies for staff training and removal expenses. France is divided into five zones. Not all incentives are available in all zones. The fifth zone, covering Paris, is purely negative in that a special tax may be imposed on the creation or extension of facilities there. The only areas to qualify for all the incentives are Corsica, and most of western, central and south-west France where the economy is basically agricultural rather than industrial.

Raising Capital locally

A number of institutions make long-term investment loans. They include the Crédit National, the Fonds de Developpement Economique et Social and the Sociétés de Developpement Régional. Short- and medium-term loans are generally made available by commercial banks. For borrowing purposes French or Dutch holding companies are often established to avoid French exchange control restrictions on non-resident borrowings. For Americans doing business in several countries, Holland would be best because of the favorable tax treaty situation.

Stock Exchange

The Stock Exchange (Bourse) is a specialized source for obtaining capital. The Paris Bourse is the largest in Europe after London. The French equivalent to the SEC is the COB (Commission des Operations de Bourse). However, it has little impact on the market as it has no power to enforce its recommendations.

In France, stock exchanges are public institutions supervised by the Ministry of Finance, and under the control of the Board of Stock Exchange Transactions.

Other exchanges in the larger cities are generally devoted to regional financial markets. There are 200,000 businesses in France but the Paris Bourse only has about 800 companies listed, all of which combined are not the equal of IBM.

Stock exchange listing usually requires sponsorship by a bank. Listing is granted by the COB after receiving the advice of the Stockbrokers Committee (*Chambre Syndicate des Agents de Changes*). There are no clearly defined requirements for listing, and acceptance

111

depends mainly on the potential market interest in the issue. However, the following factors are considered:

1. Capital of the company. The usual minimum is F.Fr. 10 million.
2. Profits during the previous four or five years.
3. Sufficient distribution of dividends.
4. Free negotiability of shares. For example, the by-laws may not contain a provision requiring the board of directors to approve of the transfer of shares.

The factors listed above apply to foreign as well as to domestic companies. Foreign companies must be listed on an official exchange in their own country. Listed companies are required to publish their annual statements in a prescribed form.

Mergers and Acquisitions

A merged company loses its existence in France. This creates valuation problems.

Acquisitions of public companies must be done through a broker (it is a criminal offense to violate this rule) with strict disclosure and accounting procedures and under the supervision of the Chambre Syndicale of the Stock Exchange.

Care must be taken when acquiring small companies that the tax authorities do not consider it to have been dissolved and its assets sold. This could have very unfavorable tax consequences.

Labor

France has a highly skilled work force and about $1\frac{1}{2}$ million foreign workers. The government supports technical training programs.

Fringe benefits can add 35% to an employe's pay.

Payroll Taxes

Employers who pay VAT on at least 90% of their gross receipts (that means most of them) are exempt from payroll tax. However, new tax laws will change this to conform to Common Market practice over the next few years.

Standard practice calls for an annual bonus of one month's pay and three weeks paid vacation.

The standard work week is 40 hours and the maximum permitted by law is 54. Penalties are imposed for overtime employment beyond the 54-hour limit.

All workers are protected by a Labor Code (*Code de Travail*). About 25% of the work force is employed by the government. The trade unions are powerful.

Work permits for foreigners are easy to obtain (*carte de travail*).

Foreigners must get a residence permit (*carte de sejour*) and managers a foreign tradesman's card (*carte d'indentité commercant etranger*).

Patents Trade marks and Copyrights
Manufacturers and traders are advised to patent their inventions and register their trademarks in France. Applications should be made through a patent or trademark agent either in France or abroad.

France sunscribes to the International Convention for the Protection of Industrial Property, the European Convention relating to the formalities required for patent applications, and the Madrid Arrangements for the international registration of trademarks.

Patents
Application for a patent may be made by the inventor or by his assignee, whether an individual, firm or corporation. Prior to the filing date (or the Convention date) of the application, the invention must not have received sufficient publicity in France or elsewhere to enable it to be put into use.

The rights of an invention belong to the first applicant. He has the option of protecting it either by a patent for a term of 20 years; or by a utility certificate lasting six years, subject to the payment of annual renewal fees. If a patented invention is not worked in France within three years from the grant of the patent or four years from filing, whichever period expires last, or if working is interrupted for more than three consecutive years, the patentee may be ordered to grant licences to others.
Pharmaceuticals and medicines can only be protected by a patent.

The first applicant is entitled to registration and exclusive use of a mark.

Registration lasts for a period of 70 years and may be renewed for similar periods. Application for renewal should be made before the expiration of the previos period of registration. If a registered trademark is not used for a period of five years, without good reason, the registration may be cancelled.

Copyrights
Copyrights exist for 50 years after the death of the author.

VII MONACO

Monaco is located on the posh Cote d'Azur surrounded by France to
the north and the Mediterranean on the south.

The Principality of Monaco is a constitutional monarchy. The
organization of the executive, legislative and judiciary powers is under
the exclusive authority of the Prince. Monaco has many links with
France. It covers an area of 435 acres and has a population
of about 24,000.

The legislature is composed of two authorities, the Prince and the
National Council. The Prince is the sole source of law.

The Principality is governed by the Prince through a Minister of
State, assisted by the Council of Government. The Minister of State,
and the three Councillors who constitute the Council of Government,
are appointed and dismissed by the Prince, to whom they are solely
responsible.

Judicial power belongs to the Prince who delegates power to the courts
which exercise the Constitution on his behalf. The Judiciary is the
responsibility of the Director of the Judiciary, who is appointed and
dismissed by the Prince.

Admission and Residence

Under an agreement with France, foreign nationals wanting to enter
Monaco must be in possession of the same documents which are required
for entry into France. Non-residents may reside there for three months.
If they wish to stay longer they should apply to the "Surete Publique"
for an identity card.

Exchange Control

Monaco is subject to French exchange control regulations.

Companies

The charter of a company must be drawn up by a lawyer (notaire),
established in Monaco, who will also file the application for
authorization.

Companies should have a capital of at least F.Fr. 100,000. Shares
must be fully paid for when issued.

The nationality of shareholders and members of the board of directors
is immaterial. The chairman of the board, or the managing director

115

(chief executive) of a company should preferably establish permanent residence in Monaco.

Branches

Applications for authorization to open a branch, or to establish a division of a foreign company, should be filed with the Minister of State.

Taxation

Companies   The only direct tax is the 35% tax on profits. This applies to profits earned by:

1. Business concerns of all types, *operating on the Monegasque territory*, with at least 25% of their turnover coming from business with foreign countries.

2. Companies collecting royalties in Monaco on patents, trademarks, processes or technical know-how, or copyrights.

Taxation of companies operating outside Monaco

Branches or headquarters of companies without significant business activity in Monaco, are not subject to profits tax. If the profits from their activities in Monaco cannot be determined, the tax is assessed at 8% of overall operating costs.

Taxation of private individuals

French subjects who transfer their regular homes to Monaco or who cannot give proof of five years of residence in Monaco prior to October 13, 1962, are subject to French income tax.

Indirect taxes

a.   Value-Added Tax
Same as France.

b.   Banking or Financing Operations
Banking, financing and securities operations are subject to a special tax calculated on gross profit at the rate of 17.6%. They are exempt from the tax on increased value.

c.   Excise Duty
A number of products such as wines, alcoholic beverages, cereals, are subject to an indirect duty on manufacture, transportation and consumption.

d.   Registration Fee
This is payable on a change of ownership of a private house. There is a registration fee of 6.50% and a transfer fee of 1.00% for a total of $7\frac{1}{2}$%. On the change of ownership of a business a 7.50% tax is also imposed.

VIII GERMANY

West Germany

BUNDESREPUBLI

DEUTSCHLAND

1 black
2 red
3 yellow

Total population 61,473,000

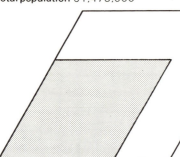

Area 95,633 sq ms / 248,469 sq kms

Population density 643 per sq m / 247 per sq km

 Form of government Federal parliamentary democracy. Executive power is vested in the Federal Government and Chancellor (Prime Minister). Federal Ministers are appointed and dismissed by the President upon proposals by the Chancellor. Legislative power is exercised by the Bundestag (Federal Parliament) and the Bundesrat (Federal Council). The Bundestag is elected for 4 years by direct, universal, and equal suffrage. The Bundesrat comprises members of the Lander governments.

 Head of state The President / elect for 5 years by a specially formed Federal Assembly

 Voting age 18 years

 Public health Compulsory contributory state insurance 99,654 doctors (1970) 683,254 hospital beds

 Major imports Raw materials, minerals, chemical products, fuel

Major exports Motor vehicles, machinery, steel, ships, chemical products, electrical products

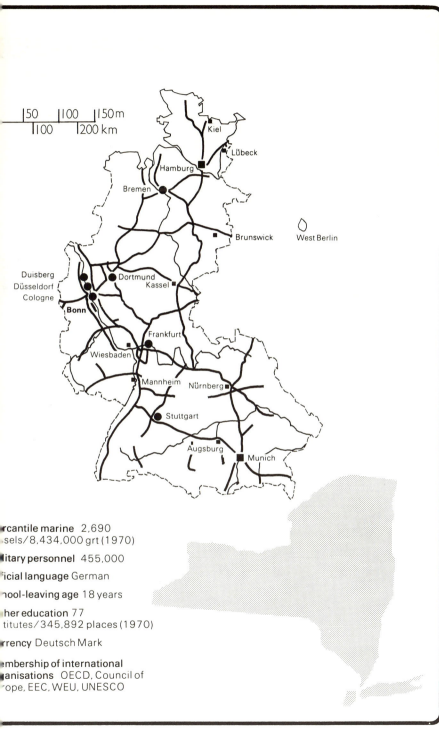

|50 |100 |150m
|100 |200 km

Kiel

Lübeck

Hamburg

Bremen

Brunswick

West Berlin

Duisberg
Düsseldorf
Cologne

Dortmund
Kassel

Bonn

Frankfurt

Wiesbaden

Mannheim   Nürnberg

Stuttgart

Augsburg

Munich

rcantile marine 2,690
sels/8,434,000 grt (1970)

itary personnel 455,000

icial language German

nool-leaving age 18 years

her education 77
titutes/345,892 places (1970)

rrency Deutsch Mark

mbership of international
anisations OECD, Council of
ope, EEC, WEU, UNESCO

The Not So Wild West

West Germany, or the Federal Republic of Germany, is a federation of ten states, created when Germany was partitioned by the "Big Four" after World War II. East Germany is now under the communist rule of the "German Democratic Republic". The old capital, Berlin, is also divided. West Berlin has a special status and is a self-governing adjunct of West Germany.

West Germany has a population of over 61 million (the largest in the Common Market), and a land area of almost 96,000 square miles. Twenty-five per cent of the population live in the industrial Ruhr area in the western part of the country.

Northern Germany is flat. The central sectors are undulating and flow into the southern mountain regions which include the Black and Bohemian forests, and the Bavarian Alps.

Germany is bordered by Belgium, Luxembourg, Czechoslovakia, Switzerland, Austria and Holland. Its communications, rail and air services are excellent. Its roads (autobahns) are the best in Europe. English is spoken in most major commercial centers and English-speaking schools exist in a number of areas.

The country is rich in natural resources including coal, iron ore, zinc, lead, copper and potash. Excellent soil and rainfall make its harvests sufficient to supply 60% of its food requirements.

There are 58 cities or towns in the Federal Republic with a population of over 100,000. Its largest city is West Berlin, with a population of 2.1 million.

Hamburg is the largest city in the main part of the Federal Republic, with a population of about 2 million. It is the third largest port in Europe and a major center for ship-building, shipping and commerce. Hamburg is also the center of the German commodity business, and a major trading center.

Hanover is probably most famous for its annual trade fair, the largest industrial exhibition of its kind in Europe. It offers the opportunity for foreign businessmen to make German business contacts and to learn about developments in German industry.

The Ruhr area remains the industrial heart of West Germany. Its coal industry has been in a decline and the big steel firms have been increasingly seeking locations outside this region for expansion. The Ruhr is deep inland. While it is served by canals and the Rhine, it is not the best place for an industry involved in foreign trade.

Frankfurt is a city which is increasingly attracting foreign businesses because of its excellent geographical position. It is within easy autobahn reach of most other German cities and has the country's largest international airport. Frankfurt is the home of the German Federal Bank and it is one of the most important banking centers in Europe.

Stuttgart and Munich, in the south, are cities of growing industrial significance. The southern part of West Germany is rapidly expanding as an industrial area and to some extent it has been neglected by foreign business. Communications by road, rail and air are good and the surrounding Bavarian countryside is probably the most delightful in Germany.

The U.S. is Germany's fourth largest trading partner and its No. 1 foreign investor (about 165 billion dollars).

Germany was rebuilt after World War II largely with U.S. money.

Since 1948, West Germany has experienced spectacular industrial and commercial growth. It ranks after the U.S., Russia and Japan as an industrial power.

In 1971, West Germany's exports were 12.6% of the world total and its share of imports was 10.5%. The major exports are machinery, motor vehicles, chemicals, iron and steel. West Germany is a major importer of metals, petroleum products, chemicals, textiles, fruit and vegetables.

The most powerful "ad" media in Germany are newspapers and magazines. Television is also widely used as it reaches 80% of German homes. Direct mail campaigns are often used. German businesses allocate proportionately larger amounts to advertising than most other Common Market countries, and foreign businessmen should anticipate similar expenditures to promote their products.

Government
Although Germany is a Federal Republic, under its Constitution

(Grundgesetz), considerable power is wielded by the 10 constituent federated States (Länder) and West Berlin. The Länder can also exercise, through the Upper Legislative House (the Bundesrat), a direct influence on the Federal Government. The Federal lower house (Bundestag) is elected partly by popular vote and partly by proportional representation. The Bundesrat's 45 members are appointed by the individual Länder Governments and are bound by their instructions. This is particularly important in the case of financial legislation which must have the express approval of the Bundesrat before it can become law. Income and corporation taxes are collected by the Länder and divided between the Länder and the Federal Government.

West Germany's head of state is the President (Bundespräsident) but the real executive power is held by the Chancellor. He is usually the leader of the majority party in the Bundestag.

The most important Federal Ministries dealing with economics and finance are the Ministerium für Wirtschaft (labor) and the Ministerium der Finanzen (finance).

Each State has its own Ministerpräsident and its own cabinet. The State cabinets always include finance and economics ministers corresponding to those in the Federal Government.

Below the Länder are a multitude of county and municipal governments which are accountable to the Länder.

Legal System

The German legal system is complex. There are separate courts in each German state for tax, administrative law, labor, social security and ordinary civil and criminal matters. Each state has its own appeal courts. Matters which go beyond the Länder courts of appeal go to Federal courts of appeal.

A special Federal Constitutional Court, the highest court in the land, has exclusive jurisdiction to guard and to interpret the Constitution (and sometimes to resolve the conflicting decisions of the High State Courts).

There is another Federal court organization consisting of the leading jurists in the Federal Court system whose function is to assure that Federal law is applied equally throughout Germany.

General Business Pointers

Hours of Business

Banks: Various, eg. 08:30 or 09:00–14:00, 08:30 or 09:00–12:00 and 14:00–15:30 Monday to Friday.

Most banks remain open until as late as 18:00 on Thursday. German banks are closed every Saturday, but a foreign exchange counter is often open at airports and on main railway stations outside normal banking hours.

Government Offices: 08:00–17:00 Monday to Friday. (Closed on Fridays at 15:30 in the Bonn area.)

Offices and Factories: Usually 08:00–17:30 (although in some parts of the country the hours will vary between half an hour and an hour).

Most business houses are closed on Saturday. Friday, especially the afternoon, is not a convenient time to call on business contacts unless invited to do so.

Shops and Post Offices: Usually 08:00 or 09:00–18:00 (some are open until 19:00; small shops and post offices may close for lunch between 13:00 and 15:00).

Most shops close at 14:00 on Saturdays except on the first Saturday of each month when many remain open until 18:00.

Official Public Vacations:

The official public and regional vacation in Germany are as follows:

New Year's Day
Epiphany—Baden Württemberg and Bavaria only
Rosenmontag—North Rhine, Westphalia only
Shrove Tuesday—Hessen and Baden Würtemberg only
Maundy Thursday—Baden Würtemberg only
Good Friday
Easter Monday
May Day
Ascension Day
Whit Monday
Waeldchestag (June 4)—Hessen only
Corpus Christi (June 13)—Except Berlin, Hamburg and Hanover
Berlin Day (June 17)
Assumption Day
Bank Holiday—Embassy and Consulates General
All Saints' Day (November 1)—Except Berlin, Hamburg and Hanover
Day of Repentance and prayers (November 21)
Christmas Day
Second Day of Christmas

Currency and Banking

The German currency is the Deutschemark (DM), which is divided into 100 pfennigs.

Banking is under the control of the Deutsches Bundesbank (German Federal Bank).

Germany has a full range of banking services although until recently it lagged behind other countries in establishing overseas banking offices. German banks are usually organized on a regional basis.

Branches of foreign banks, once licensed, are treated as German

123

institutions. Foreign banks establishing a subsidiary have to bring in a minimum capital of DM 3 million.

32 of the world's 300 largest banks are German. The four largest commercial banks in order of assets are: Deutsche Bank, Dresdner Bank, Westdeutsche Landesbank Girozentrale and Commerzbank.

The "Giro" system is widely used for transfers between bank accounts. Every holder of a bank account can use the giro payment procedure which is both inexpensive and safe since it merely involves bank transfer orders. Payment by personal checks is not common in Germany.

Banks do not normally return paid checks but do send the account holder a statement whenever there is a movement in his account.

Banks have a service for clients who own bearer shares of German companies. They arrange for collection of dividends, obtain copies of annual accounts and notice of meetings, and act as proxies.

Exchange Control

Germany has had to impose temporary exchange controls on a number of occasions over the recent past. This has been necessary to curb heavy inflows of funds from abroad. Most of these controls were lifted following the U.S. decision to end the interest equalization tax. But if the DM comes under renewed upward pressure the West German government may be forced to impose controls once again.

Non-residents can buy most types of German shares and bonds without restriction.

Restrictions are placed on funds borrowed abroad to finance a German company. Cash deposit regulations (the "bardepot") require German residents, including subsidiaries and branches of foreign companies, to place on deposit with the Central Bank 20% of funds borrowed from abroad. These deposits earn no interest.

Foreign investors have three alternatives when buying or setting up a company in Germany.

1. They can either borrow the funds in Germany. This is often difficult and quite expensive.

2. Borrow the funds abroad and make a large investment in the German venture. This may pose problems. If the amount of capital is not related to the size of the business, part of the capital could be considered as "borrowings" and become subject to the "bardepot".

3. Make a form of capital contribution to their subsidiaries which is not subject to the cash deposit law.

There are no barriers to repatriation of capital, dividends, interest, license fees and royalties. The transfer of such funds can be arranged through any bank.

124   All businesses in West Germany are required to make monthly

returns to their state bank (Landeszentralbank) of figures of foreign debtors, creditors, and deposits. Penalties are imposed for failure to comply with these regulations.

Import-Export

There are no special exchange control requirements on imports and exports. Imports may be paid for in any convertible currency and all banks in the Federal Republic can carry out foreign exchange transactions.

There is no time limit for payments to be made even when the transaction is subject to import license regulations.

Importers have to submit an import declaration to the nearest branch of the Bundesbank within 14 days of signing the contract. This is needed for customs control and statistical purposes only.

There are Duty Free Ports in Hamburg, Bremen and Bremerhaven, which offer businessmen and governments an area free of duties, customs formalities and unnecessary restrictions. A free port user may send his cargo directly to warehouses where the goods may be stored, processed, assembled, packaged, re-built and trans-shipped to the market. No matter how long goods are left at the free port duties are not levied. Warehouse charges are moderate and competitive. Goods imported into Germany are subject to duty and tax when they leave the free port.

The German tariff is based on the Brussels nomenclature system of classification. Nearly all duties are on an 'ad valorem' basis.

Forms of Doing Business

The type of company you use in Germany depends basically on the size and nature of the business to be carried out. The following are the main types of organization possible:

a. a branch office (Zweigniederlassung);
b. sole trader (Einzelfirma);
c. ordinary commercial partnership (offene Handelsgesellschaft) (OHG);
d. limited partnership (Kommanditgesellschaft) (KG);
e. limited partnership with a private limited company as the only fully liable partner (GmbH & Co KG);
f. private limited company (Gesellschaft mit beschrankter Haftung) (GmbH);
g. public limited company (Aktiengesellschaft) (AG).

In practice, the choice for a foreign firm lies between a branch office, a public limited company (AG), a private limited company (GmbH), and the possibility of buying an interest in an existing German company.

125

Branch Office (Zweigniederlassung)

German law permits a foreign company or partnership to set up a branch. A branch cannot be independent of the parent company. There are certain disadvantages in setting up a branch office:

a. To go into business under its own name in Germany a foreign corporation needs a license from the Ministry of Economics and it is advisable to obtain it before the branch is opened.

b. A Zweidniederlassung is a branch which is sufficiently self-contained to be able to operate independently from the head office. Small branches are therefore unlikely to be registered. A Zweigniederlassung must be entered in the Commercial Register of the local court where the branch is established. The court requires a sworn and notarized copy of the constitution of the parent company and other supporting documents. It then undertakes a detailed investigation of whether the organization of the foreign company meets with the German legal requirements. Registration usually takes at least six months and can take up to 12 months. It can therefore be an expensive operation in terms of time and legal fees.

c. Under double taxation agreements, a branch is usually held to be a permanent establishment of the parent company. It is taxed on that part of the branch's profits earned in Germany.

A branch is generally taxed less favorably than a GmbH or other corporate entity. Foreign firms should try to avoid carrying out business in Germany through a branch office.

Public Limited Liability Company

At least five founder-shareholders are needed to form an AG company. AG's must have a minimum share capital of DM 100,000 of which at least 25% must be paid in at incorporation. The founders may be personally liable for pre-incorporation debts though these may be assumed by the company after formation. Shares in the AG must have a minimum par value of DM 50. Shares are normally in bearer form. Shareholders may be individuals or corporations and may be residents of any country.

An AG has a two-tier management structure. The board of managers (vorstand) carries out the day-to-day managerial operations and a supervisory board of directors (the aufsichtstrat) acts in a more general advisory capacity. The two boards have separate functions and members. The supervisory board of directors represents the owners, appoints the vorstand and also sets their salaries, bonuses and term of employment (normally five years). Appointees need not be shareholders. The vorstand, in turn, is permitted to establish rules on its voting methods, meetings and other administrative matters. If the AG share capital is over DM 3 million the vorstand board must have at least two members.

There may be from 3 to 21 supervisory managers, depending on the company's size. They are appointed by the founder-shareholders and thereafter are elected at subsequent shareholder meetings. At least one-third of the directors must be elected by the employees of the AG. (This innovation has provided excellent labor relations for a number of years). This board appoints and supervises the board of managers and may assume additional duties as provided in the Articles of Incorporation.

There must be an annual shareholders' meeting. The shareholders have power to appoint and dismiss members from both managerial boards (except for those elected by the workers), as well as amend the company's articles, approve mergers, make changes in capital, take decisions to liquidate and other matters.

The managers may appoint 'prokuristen' who are given special powers to represent the company in day-today affairs. Their transactions with third parties are generally binding on the company. Their names must be on the Commercial Register and the initials 'ppa' must precede their signature. Limited authority to act on behalf of the company may be given to employees who are called 'handelsbevollmachtigter'.

Private Limited Liability Company (GmbH)

The GmbH is a simpler corporate structure and subject to fewer regulations than the AG. For this reason many foreign firms choose this form.

The GmbH requires only two founding partners who may be individuals or corporations. One of these may be a nominee who after formation transfers his share to his principal. The Articles of Association must be prepared by a notary public. Minimum capital required is DM 20,000 and the minimum individual shareholding is DM 500. At least 25% must be paid in.

The GmbH does not issue share certificates. Its stock is non-negotiable and may be transferred only by notarial deed. It may not issue bonds.

Unless the number of the GmbH's employees exceeds 500 it is not required to have a supervisory board. The GmbH is run by one or more managers who do not have to be German citizens, residents or shareholders of the company. They are responsible to the shareholders who may fix their salaries or restrict their managerial authority.

The registration of a new GmbH takes from two to four months.

Acquisitions

It is possible to acquire an existing business entity. This saves time and expense. Under German tax laws a loss in the German company

127

cannot be transferred to the buyer. This reduces the advantage in acquiring an existing company.

Partnerships

The main partnership forms are the general partnership (offene handelsgesellschaft, or OHG) and the limited partnership (kommanditgesellschaft or KG). Partners in the OHG are personally liable for partnership debts. In the KG there is at least one general partner with full personal liability and inactive partners whose liability is limited to their investments. A special type of KG exists called GmbH and Co. KG. In this case a GmbH may be the general partner and its shareholders the limited partners.

Rules on Foreign-owned Businesses

While there are special formalities for foreign-owned businesses, a foreign enterprise can freely establish itself in Germany. Before a foreign company can commence business or acquire an exisiting business, it must:

1.   Report to the local supervisory agency for business and trade (an office of the state Ministry of Economics). This office decides if there are any reasons to bar the enterprise. If a foreign company (from other than an EEC country) wants to set up a branch it must show that it meets the minimum capital requirements applicable to comparable German companies. The foreign company must submit with its application, a copy of its last three annual accounts, and details of its directors and branch managers. All of these documents must be translated into German.

2. Report to the municipal trade tax office, the local office of the federal tax authority and the local social security office and pay a capital transactions tax. Once paid, the enterprise must be registered in the Commercial Register (Handelsregister) of the local court (Amtsgerichte). It will receive a registration number.

3. If the investment is to exceed the value of DM 10,000 per year, the company must submit a report to central bank of the state concerned (Landeszentralbank).

There are special restrictions concerning certain trades such as foods, pharmaceuticals, banks and insurance.

Resident representatives responsible for the business must be designated. A foreign manager need not reside in West Germany. After formation the enterprise need only conform to the regulations applicable to all businesses in West Germany.

All businesses must join the local Chamber of Commerce.

Foreign firms frequently do business in Germany through agents and distributors. Such firms must be careful not to create a "permanent establishment" for tax purposes in Germany. The most popular form is a "commission agency". However, German law grants the agent strong protection in case of termination of the agency. It is advisable for foreign businesses to have their agency agreements drafted by lawyers with expertise in this area. This word of caution also applies to dealers who import for their own accounts.

Letterheads of German business organizations must indicate their legal form, capital, registration number and names of their managers. Customarily the name of the firm's bank and its account number are also shown.

Taxes

The taxes imposed in West Germany are:
Personal income and corporation tax
Trade tax
Value-added tax
Inheritance and gift tax
Withholding tax on dividends and distributions
Net wealth tax

Corporate Tax

Corporations resident in Germany are taxable on their world wide net income. A company is resident if incorporated in the Federal Republic or if its central place of management is in West Germany (even if the business is incorporated in another country). Non-resident businesses are taxed on profits earned by a permanent establishment in the Federal Republic.

All business income is considered profit and is calculated on the increase or decrease of the taxpayer's net worth during the year. The annual opening and closing balance sheets are compared to arrive at this figure. The tax laws specify detailed valuation rules as taxable income will be affected by balance sheet valuations of assets and liabilities. Some firms find it necessary to prepare special balance sheets for tax purposes.

Fixed income producing assets must be depreciated each year regardless of the amount of income they produce. Assets are written off according to their useful life and potential obsolescence. Replacement value is not considered in computing depreciation. Both "straight line" and declining balance methods may be used. If declining balance is chosen the rate of write-off cannot exceed twice the amount the straight line method would yield and in any case not be more than 20% of the assets' value. Buildings can only be treated with straight line depreciation.

There is some flexibility on the actual rates and periods of depreciation   129 allowed and these can be negotiated with the tax authorities.

Assets receiving unusual wear and tear may qualify for accelerated depreciation.

Goodwill and other intangible assets may only be capitalized if purchased. These assets must be amortized over a five year period. This amortization is tax deductible only if there has been a decline in inherent value.

Most taxes paid by a corporation are tax deductible except for corporation and net wealth taxes. Other deductible items include interest, royalty fees, bad debts, remuneration to directors and shareholders (except that amounts paid to the supervisory directors are not deductible), and organizational expenses.

Special deductions are granted for investments in developing countries and certain reserve accounts can be utilized for tax deferral. Profit sharing bonuses are deductible as well as pension contributions by employees if special conditions are met.

Expenses for entertainment such as maintenance of yachts or guest houses for hunting or fishing which are not located in the area of the business are disallowed as deductions.

Dividend Income

A 25% withholding tax is taken from dividends paid to both resident and non-resident shareholders. These dividend contributions are not deductible for corporate tax purposes. Double taxation agreements may grant a lower withholding rate. The applicable rate for U.S. residents is 15% if the recipient owns 10% or more of the German company—otherwise the rate is 25%.

A corporation pays no tax on dividends received if both the paying and and recipient company are German resident companies and 25% of the shares of the payor are owned by the recipient for the previous 12 months. However, unless the recipient company redistributes the dividends to its shareholders, a 36% supplementary tax will be levied against this income. Such distributions will only qualify for tax avoidance if the company has made a total distribution of its own profits for the year.

The 25% tax on dividends, interest, royalties and other distributions, received by non-resident individuals and corporations, is collected at its source or by assessment.

Foreign dividends received by a resident company are liable to corporate tax. This tax may be partially exempted by treaty if the German company holds a substantial interest in the foreign distributor.

An interesting feature of German tax law concerns taxation of a group of companies. It allows the total profit and losses of a controlled subsidiary to be pooled with the parent's income. This procedure requires that the parent holds, directly or indirectly, 50% of the voting rights in the subsidiary, and that it controls the subsidiary. The parent must also receive the profits, or be liable for the losses, of the subsidiary for five years.

Capital gains are treated as ordinary income and taxed accordingly. Capital losses are deductible.

Losses can be carried forward five years but "carry backs" are disallowed. The carry over does not survive a merger or a change in the corporation's business.

A non-resident branch which maintains a permanent establishment in Germany is taxed on its German source income at a set rate of 50.47%, including surcharge. The branch is required to keep its accounting records in Germany. Deductions are not permitted for payments to the foreign headquarters for interest, royalties and "know-how". If the German branch does business in third countries it cannot deduct taxes it pays in these countries nor credit the foreign tax against its West German corporation tax.

Non-residents are taxed at the standard 50.47% rate on interest from loans secured by a mortgage on property in West Germany. Other interest income is not taxed. Some double tax treaties provide reduced or nil rates of tax for dividends, interest and royalties but not in the case of the U.S. U.S. royalties are taxed at the 25% withholding rate.

Profits remitted by a branch to its parent are not subject to withholding tax.

Foreign tax credit is usually available for foreign source income taxed in Germany.

The basic resident corporate tax rate is 52.53% on undistributed profits and 15.45% on profits paid out as dividends. These figures include a 3% surcharge.

Companies whose nominal capital is owned 76% by individuals and whose assets are less than DM 5 million, may pay a graduated tax with an optimum rate of 50.47% on retained profits over DM 50,000 rather than the normal rates. The effective tax rate on distributed income under the optional scale is 27.3%. A decision to pay the normal rate applies for five years.

The usual tax year is the calendar year, and the normal tax due date is May 30. Some extension is permissible but seriously overdue returns may be penalized up to 10% of the tax charged for the year.

Tax on Individuals

German residents are taxable on their world wide income and non-residents on income from German sources. Tax treaties may vary the tax charged.

Residents are individuals whose customary home is in the Federal

131

Republic. An individual resident in Germany for six months in any 12-month period is considered a resident.

A number of tax treaties grant foreign employees, resident in Germany less than 183 days of a tax year, an exemption on their earned income. To qualify they must receive their pay from non-resident employers. This payment cannot be claimed as a tax deduction on the employer's tax returns in Germany.

Germany has tax treaties with most of the industrialized nations of the world.

Individuals who take up residence and are considered specially valuable to Germany can negotiate annual lump sum tax payments in lieu of normal taxes for periods up to ten years.

Individuals are taxed on earned income, capital and investment, rentals, profits from business, trade or personal services and from agricultural and industrial sources.

Gross income is the aggregate gain from all of these categories. The taxable total is arrived at by allowing for income-connected expenses, personal allowances and other exemptions. Individuals are free from tax on capital gains arising from property held over two years and other assets held for over six months. Otherwise the appropriate ordinary tax is paid. Gain from an individual's business-related capital assets are taxed at standard rates.

Individuals can claim tax allowances on trade union fees, professional association subscriptions, cost of professional or vocational tools, journals, working clothes, and the cost of travel to and from work. A standard DM 564 employment expense deduction is allowed. Higher amounts must be substantiated.

Deductions are also allowed for special personal expenses such as interest and annuities connected with an income source, insurance premiums, and charitable gifts.

Child allowances for the first, second and each subsequent child are DM 1,200, DM 1,680, and DM 1,800 respectively. There are also old age allowances and accident and illness deductions.

Non-residents are allowed a deduction of DM 840 in lieu of personal exemptions and allowances.

Tax Reform

German tax reforms are aimed at helping those on low incomes. Deductions and exemptions are being increased so that while the minimum tax rate rises only the higher wage earners are affected. These progressive tax rates will run from 30% to 56%.

Income from the sale of an entirely unincorporated business or sale of shares by a "substantial shareholder" is taxed at one-half of the average rate paid on an individual's total taxable income.

A wage tax is withheld and paid by the employer.

The Brandt Administration adopted the tax credit principle on corporate taxation.

There is also a municipal trade tax on income, capital and the payrolls of commercial enterprises.

Value-Added Tax

VAT (Mehrwertstever) is charged on goods and services within Germany. Exempted items include leasing of land and housing, physicians and hospital services, banking and monetary operations and exports.

The VAT rate is 11% with a reduced rate of 5.5% for foodstuffs, special items and certain professional services. The tax is levied on the net price paid for goods or services. It must be itemized separately on any invoice over DM 50.

VAT is generally assessed at the end of the calendar year. The business or individual must file a monthly declaration within ten days after the end of each month. A yearly return is submitted at the end of each calendar year.

Delivery is considered executed at the place where the power of disposition passes; or, for shipped goods, where the shipment originated. Services include activities such as leasing equipment, licensing patents, and professional services.

There is no VAT on imports, but there is an 11% import turnover tax charged on the customs value. The tax is charged regardless of whether the goods are dutiable.

Special VAT rates apply to small businesses.

Businesses with an annual turnover not in excess of DM 12,000 are tax exempt. Annual turnover amounting to more than DM 12,000 and not exceeding DM 60,000 is subject to a turnover tax (not VAT) at the rate of 4% on the invoiced amount. This tax cannot be credited by the customer and must not be shown in the invoice of the supplier. This exemption may be waived by the tax-payer in favor of the normal VAT system in order to facilitate a claim for tax credit.

Other taxes

There is a 1% net wealth tax levied on total net worth of assets of individuals and companies. Non-residents are liable only for German assets and residents are allowed liberal exemptions in computation of this tax.

A capital transactions tax of 2% is charged on the formation or increase in capital of a company, on contributions by a foreign company to assets of its branch or subsidiary, on the first acquisition of shares in a German company and similar transactions.

133

Regulations:

Germany has the most regulated commercial sector in the Common Market. Care must be taken to know the law relative to your business activities.

If German words appear on goods, the country of origin must be stated. The German Foodstuffs Marking Order (Lebensmittel-Kennzeichnungsverordnung) regulates price markings on retail goods.

The Prepackaging Order (Fertigpackungsverordnung) regulates the sizes, pricing and contents marking of prepacked consumer goods. The Textile Marking Law (Textilkennzeichnungsgesetz) requires the raw material content to be shown on the textile products. Translations of these laws are available from the OTAR section of the Export Services and Promotions Division.

Exporters of foodstuffs to Germany should consult the Foodstuffs Law (Lebensmittelgesetz). Drugs or medicines imported into Germany for sale to the public must conform to the Federal Medicaments Law (Arzneimittelgesetz). This lays rules on composition, packing, labelling, registration as branded medicine (Arzneispezialitaet) and other information. Enquiries should be addressed to the Federal Ministry of Health (Bundesgesundheitministerium), 53 Bonn-Bad Godesburg, Kennedy Alle 105-107.

Real Estate

There are no restrictions on the acquisition of property by foreigners.

Stock Market

The Frankfurt Stock Exchange is the largest in West Germany but German stock markets are small.

Bond issues require the approval of the Federal Ministry of Economics. Other securities may be issued without government approval.

A prospectus is required to obtain a stock market listing. It must be published in the Federal Gazette and one newspaper. Company accounts for the last three years must be submitted to the Stock Exchange.

Business Incentives

Businesses and individuals resident in West Berlin are granted special tax rates. Companies with their principal place of business in West Berlin or who have a permanent establishment there employing a minimum of 25 persons receive a 20% corporate tax reduction on their West Berlin income. They are also given an additional tax credit equal to 3.2% of West Berlin income. Accelerated depreciation of 75% on cost of equipment and 50% on buildings is also allowed. Individuals have a 30% income tax reduction on West Berlin earnings. VAT is reduced by 4.5% for deliveries to West Germany and by 6% for certain services. A West German customer also is permitted to reduce the VAT payable by him to 4.2%. There are also special rates to encourage capital investments in West Berlin.

Labor

There is little unemployment in West Germany. It has the largest labor force in the EEC (12 million). There are over 2.5 million foreign workers in West Germany. New firms can expect difficulties recruiting staff. It is common for employment contracts to contain provisions limiting workers from joining competitive firms within a specified period of time.

Wages and working conditions in Germany are governed by collective agreements between employers' associations and labor unions covering the whole of an industry in the country or in a particular Land (state). These agreements can be declared binding on firms and workers in the industry.

The legal standard working week is $5\frac{1}{2}$ days, or 48 hours for manual and office workers. But this now by large a fiction and the 5-day week is practically universal. The average actually worked is about 42 hours for men and 39 for women in industry, and rather less in commerce. The trend is downwards, and collective agreements with some unions provide for a shorter working week in many industries. Overtime work is normally paid 25% extra. Manual and office workers are entitled to paid vacations of 15 to 24 days a year, depending on age and length of service.

Female workers are generally prohibited from night work, and may not work six weeks before and after childbirth or be dismissed during this time. Their compensation for this 12 weeks period is based on their average earnings. Children under 14 usually cannot be employed.

Generally speaking, executives and qualified staff will expect to be paid more than their counterparts in the U.S. The rates vary widely according to industries, areas and size of organization.

Fringe benefits vary widely. A "13 month" salary is common. Vacations and six weeks sick allowance per year are paid. Many firms offer share options, savings schemes and other incentives.

Unions are strong and well-organized. The country's strike record is the lowest in Europe and wildcat or unofficial strikes are rare.

Patents, Trademarks and Copyrights

Foreign nationals have equal rights with Germans for patent, trade-mark and copyright protection. Germany is a member of the important national treaties on these subjects.

Patents are granted for 18 years. Under the Paris convention a patent application in any signatory country establishes a one-year right of priority in the Federal Republic. Compulsory licensings may be necessary.

Trademarks are valid for 10 years and are renewable. Reservation of a trademark will be lost if it is not used within five years of its registration.

Copyright protection extends to 50 years after the author's death.

For further information about Germany contact:
Deutscher Industrie und Handelstag (DIHT)
(Federation of German Chamber of Commerce)
5300 Bonn, Adenauer Allee 148. Tel: 1041

Ausstellungs-und Messe-Ausschuss der Deutschen Wirtschaft (AUMA)
(Exhibition and Fair Committee of German Industry)
5000 Cologne, Engelbertstr. 31a. Tel: 21 90 91

IX THE UNITED KINGDOM
Channel Islands, Gibraltar, Isle of Man

UNITED KINGDOM

red cross
white border
blue triangle

Total population 55,346,551

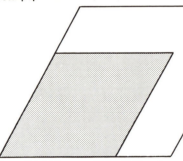

Area 94,216 sq ms/244,019 sq kms

Population density 587 per sq m/227 per sq km

 Form of government Constitutional monarchy. The Monarch is legal head of the executive but executive power is exercised by the Cabinet headed by the Prime Minister. Legislative authority is vested in the Monarch and Parliament, comprising the House of Lords and the House of Commons. The Lords sit by hereditary right or are appointed for life on the Government's recommendation. The Commons are elected by direct and universal suffrage. The lifespan of a Parliament is limited to 5 years.

 Head of state The Monarch/hereditary succession

 Voting age 18 years

 **Public health** Compulsory contributory state insurance 52,000 doctors 533,000 hospital beds

 Major imports Raw materials, fuel foodstuffs, semi-manufactured goods, capital goods

Major exports Engineering products, motor vehicles, aircraft scientific instruments, textiles

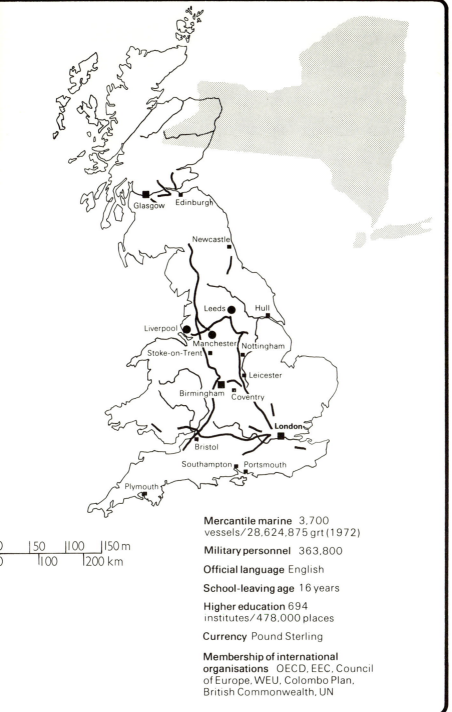

Glasgow
Edinburgh
Newcastle
Leeds Hull
Liverpool
Manchester Nottingham
Stoke-on-Trent
Leicester
Birmingham Coventry
London
Bristol
Southampton Portsmouth
Plymouth

0 | 50 | 100 | 150 m
0 | 100 | 200 km

Mercantile marine 3,700
vessels/28,624,875 grt (1972)

Military personnel 363,800

Official language English

School-leaving age 16 years

Higher education 694
institutes/478,000 places

Currency Pound Sterling

**Membership of international
organisations** OECD, EEC, Council
of Europe, WEU, Colombo Plan,
British Commonwealth, UN

© DIAGRAM

The New Battle of Britain

Americans tend to assume that England and Britain are one and the same. This is not so. England is part of Great Britain. Great Britain consists of the countries of England, Scotland and Wales. The United Kingdom is Great Britain plus Northern Ireland. The British Isles are Great Britain and Ireland but the Republic of Ireland (Eire) is not part of the United Kingdom.

The northern Irish, the southern Irish, the English, the Scots and the Welsh are all very different peoples with great ethnic pride in their individual histories and accomplishments.

The U.K. covers about 93,000 square miles. Its population is over 55 million, making it the second largest in the EEC (after Germany) and one of the most densely populated countries in the world.

About 40% of the population lives in or near major cities. London, the capital, has a population of about 10 million.

The countryside is lovely. England is basically flat, but Scotland and Wales have small mountain ranges. British farms are the most efficient in the Common Market but it is mainly an industrial state.

Britain was once the greatest power in the world. From 1588 when Sir Francis Drake destroyed the Spanish Armada, until World War II, Britain had the greatest navy in the world.

Time was when "the sun never set on the British Empire." Now all is gone and Britain is going through a very difficult period of adjustment from an insular but rich and powerful island to a poor partner in the Common Market, where it will only be respected for what it does, not what it was. Britain has seen its currency diminish in value and its balance of payments is poor. But the British have shown often their national ability to overcome and recover quickly from adversity.

However, the British do not have to rely entirely on courage and determination. London is the center of world insurance, European banking and stock market activity and major oil and gas strikes have been made in the North Sea.

Inevitably Britain must achieve a prominent position in the EEC. It was granted five years to bring its farm prices into line with other EEC countries. In its first year of EEC membership Britain got more from the

EEC Social Fund (for worker retraining) than any other country. Furthermore, Britain is the only EEC country that will be self-sufficient in oil, natural gas and coal.

Communications and transport facilities are good. London's Heathrow is the busiest airport in Europe and British Airways is its largest airline.

Until very recently Britain and the U.S. enjoyed a "special relationship." This is ending now that the U.K. is part of the EEC. Yet, after Canada, Britain receives more U.S. investment than any other country. It is estimated that up to 85% of foreign investment in Britain is from the U.S. More than half of the largest American companies have interests in the U.K. The value of U.S. controlled shares on the London Stock Exchange is about 125 billion dollars. Obviously, the language similarity (but remember—English and American are two different languages) is a spur to U.S. investment.

The British still use feet and pounds although they are switching to the metric system.

Political Structure

The treaty of 1707 established the Union between England and Scotland but both parts continue to have different systems of law, education and local government, and for most domestic matters, different government departments. The main Scottish departments are grouped under the Secretary of State for Scotland, who is a member of the U.K. Cabinet. Scotland's capital is Edinburgh.

In Northern Ireland, the law is similar to English law, but its judiciary is separate. Ulster's capital is Belfast.

There is home rule to some extent in the administration of Welsh affairs under a member of the U.K. Cabinet, the Secretary of State for Wales, who is entrusted with the task of preserving the peculiarities of Welsh life and thought.

The Channel Islands and the Isle of Man are not part of the U.K., but are Crown dependencies with special relationship status. They have their own legislative bodies, local administrations, law system, and courts. Nevertheless, the U.K. Parliament has formal jurisdiction over these dependencies except in domestic matters, which are left to the local legislative bodies.

The U.K. is a constitutional monarchy. The Crown has no real authority.

The supreme legislative authority rests with Parliament, which consists of two houses—the House of Commons, which has all the power, and the House of Lords. The House of Commons has 635 members who are elected in national elections. The membership of the House of Lords is made up of hereditary peers (Lords), life peers,

141

representative peers from Northern Ireland and Scotland, and archbishops and bishops. They hold their seats by virtue of their titles, and their function is to "assist" the House of Commons.

Either House can introduce a law but tax laws must be introduced by the House of Commons.

Parliament (The House of Commons) is elected for five years but the ruling party can call a general election at any time. The government can "fall" as a result of a "no confidence" vote. The majority party selects the Prime Minister who in turn selects his cabinet.

The U.K. is divided into 98 counties and a number of municipalities and boroughs. Local "councils" have considerable authority. Councillors are elected to office. There are plans to revamp local government.

Legal System

Britain's Common Law system formed the basis of the U.S. legal system. As Britain ruled Ireland for many years, the Irish system of law is also the same.

The British Constitution is unwritten and consists of all the laws of England. Parliament can do as it sees fit at any time without restraint. But the democratic tradition in the U.K. assures that this power will not be abused.

Separate judicial systems exist in Northern Ireland, Wales, Scotland and England. Scottish law is based on Roman law and is very different from the others. Scottish juries can return a "not proven" verdict.

The House of Lords is the highest court for all the countries.

County courts have nothing to do with counties. Like many things in Britain, the name was kept out of a sense of tradition. There are 500 county courts which deal with small matters and do not generally try contested or criminal cases.

More important is the High Court of Justice which has unlimited general jurisdiction. It also has appellate jurisdiction.

The Chancery Division deals with estates, trusts, land and business matters.

The Queen's Bench Division deals with libel, negligence, criminal appeals, shipping and similar matters.

There is also a Family Division, a Court of Appeals, and several other institutions which carry over from ancient times.

On the criminal side there are the Magistrates Courts with limited power, the Crown Court with broad power (the "Old Bailey" is a Crown Court) and courts of appeal leading to the House of Lords.

There are a number of administrative courts for tax, labor and other
matters.

General Business Pointers
Business Hours
The U.K. is on Greenwich Mean Time except from mid-March to mid-October when it is on GMT plus one hour.

Most offices open from 09:30 to 17:30, but it may be hard to find a British executive before 10:00.

Banks are open from 09:30 to 15:00.

Post offices vary but usually are open from 09:00 to 16:30 and half day on Saturday.

Vacations (England and Wales)
Britain has the fewest vacations in the EEC.

New Year's Day
Good Friday
Easter Monday
Spring Bank Holiday
Summer Bank Holiday
Christmas Day
Boxing Day

Currency and Banking
The British currency is the pound sterling. It is divided into 100 pence.

All banking is under the control of the Bank of England. There are very few rules or laws regulating banking in the U.K. The British believe they can work on the honor system.

Britain has full banking services. Its banks are more familiar with foreign affairs than the banks of any other country. They have been operating overseas for many years.

Residents may be permitted "overdrafts". This is a form of borrowing by overdrawing your account with permission from the bank.

It is the banks who fulfil most of industry's requirements for short-term finance either by way of fluctuating *"overdraft"* or short-term loan.

The largest U.K. bank, Barclays, is the fourth largest in the world and the largest non-American bank. The major British banks have a large number of offices in the U.S. and around the world.

Exchange Control
Exchange control regulations apply to most forms of investment in and the export of funds from the "Scheduled Territories" by non-residents. It is much more serious to cheat on exchange regulations than on your income tax—so beware!

The Scheduled Territories are the U.K. (including the Isle of Man and the Channel Islands) Gibraltar, and the Republic of Ireland.

143

Direct investment in the U.K. by non-residents is generally welcomed to aid the balance of payments. Bank of England permission is necessary and steps must be taken to safeguard the right of repatriation of capital. The Bank of England is usually approached through a bank but few bankers seem familiar with exchange control regulations. (Consult an accountant or lawyer in important matters.)

Individuals

Non-residents have "external accounts" which may be used freely to import or export currency.

Residents cannot export money from their bank accounts without Bank of England approval.

Sterling cannot be paid into an external account without exchange control consent.

A person can be resident in the U.K. "for exchange control purposes" even though he is not a true resident of the country. Residence for exchange control purposes usually means maintaining an external account for four years and "visiting" the U.K. for more than 90 days a year for more than three years. It is up to the U.K. banks to enforce much of the exchange control regulations but many find it too difficult to keep track of their customers. The Bank of England seems to be permissive with non-British individuals who do not go too far off base.

Branch Offices

A branch office of a non-resident company will normally be regarded for exchange control purposes as a U.K. resident. Permission is not needed to invest foreign currency in a branch office. But if any substantial amount is involved it is advisable to check with the Bank of England at an early stage to ensure that eventual repatriation of the investment will be permitted.

Limited Company

A limited company formed and registered in the U.K. will be regarded for exchange control purposes as resident in the U.K., irrespective of the domicile of the shareholders. Permission under the Exchange Control Act is needed for a company to issue shares to anyone resident outside the Scheduled Territories. This permission is normally easy to get but any subsequent finance (other than by way of ploughed-back profits) must be found from foreign sources in proportion to the non-resident stake in the company. The Bank of England will vary this rule only if the project is judged to be of exceptional benefit to the U.K.

Advance permission is needed for an investment in the form of a foreign loan whether the loan is expressed in sterling or in foreign currency. Permission will not normally be given for the U.K. branch or

144

company to accept sterling loans from non-resident sources. However, permission will usually be granted for foreign currency loans from any source which are not due for repayment within five years. This permission normally includes authority for repayment as well as the periodic payment of interest at a reasonable rate. However, where the borrowing company is controlled by non-residents the Bank of England will probably stipulate that repayment will only be permitted from the company's own financial resources.

The investment may be in any one or more of the following methods:
1. cash
2. the provision of plant, machinery or materials
3. the transfer of patent rights, technical "know-how", and the like.

Cash must be in sterling from external accounts, or in sterling derived from selling a foreign currency to a U.K. bank. If part or all of the capital is to be provided in the form of plant or equipment, any necessary import license must first be obtained from the Department of Trade and Industry. The value of patent rights has to be agreed with the Bank of England.

The authorities will allow the transfer of dividends to non-resident shareholders after U.K. tax has been paid.

U.K. residents need permission to make loans or payment to a company or person outside the Sterling Area.

Companies which are controlled by EEC or Sterling Area residents will normally be permitted to raise all the sterling finance they require. This does not apply to investment holding companies.

Companies controlled by residents outside the Scheduled Territories will normally be permitted to raise sterling finance in the U.K. if the funds are required for operations in special development areas. Other cases are dealt with on their merits. U.K. companies in which non-residents have less than a controlling interest are allowed unlimited sterling borrowing in the U.K., unless the company is purely a vehicle for portfolio investment.

Licensing and Technical Agreements

Overseas payments are allowed on patent royalties and on charges for "know-how" and technical services. So are management fees and other charges from a foreign company to its U.K. subsidiary. Evidence has to be provided to the bank through which payment is made. Special Bank of England approval is needed for payments of £50,000 and over.

Foreign Employees

An employee only temporarily in the U.K. will be regarded for exchange control purposes as a non-resident, and he will be allowed to remit his earnings abroad. These earnings will normally be subject to

U.K. tax (see section on tax). If the employee expects to live in the U.K. for at least three years, he will usually be regarded for exchange control purposes as a resident. He would then be free to receive payments from any source, but would be limited on payments abroad and the retention of foreign currencies. He would be permitted to send home up to £2,000 a year out of his U.K. earnings to support dependents. U.S. citizens and other foreigners resident in the U.K. may obtain "a measure of exemption" from exchange control regulations on assets denominated in their native currency.

A foreign employee who has been resident in the U.K. for at least three years may, on leaving the U.K., take his sterling assets with him up to £5,000, in addition to his personal and household effects. The balance can be taken over the next four years (although this rule is not strictly enforced).

Forms of Doing Business in the U.K.

Large organizations do not dominate U.K. industry. Some 80,000 manufacturing companies employing less than 200 people each represent 90% of the total number of units and nearly one-third of manufacturing output.

While there are some minor differences in the forms of business activities in various parts of the U.K., we will concentrate on the English system.

1. *Partnerships*—similar to a U.S. partnership. There can be no more than 20 partners (with some exceptions). A person or a company can be a partner. Every partner is liable not only for the company's debts but for his partner's tax liability arising from partnership income.

2. *Limited partnerships*. They must have at least one general partner and must be registered. The limited partners' liability extends only to their investment.

3. *Unlimited company*—a cross between a company and a partnership. The company is liable for its debts but the investors must make additional capital contributions upon demand. It is used mainly by banks and mutual funds.

4. *Company limited by guaranty*. Used mainly by non-profit organizations, the subscribers guarantee to pay a certain sum when the company is dissolved.

5. *Company limited by shares*. There are two types—public and private.

a. private companies are closely held

b. public companies resemble U.S. public companies.

We will concentrate on these two forms.

Formation

Forming a U.K. company is simple. Laws governing the formation of a company are contained in the Companies Act. It enables, in the case of a public company, any seven or more persons, and in the case of a private company, any two or more persons, to form a company by putting their names to a Memorandum of Association and complying with the requirements of the Companies Act. Once incorporated, the company becomes a legal entity separate and distinct from its individual members. It can then trade under its own name. The Memorandum is signed by each original subscriber and the number of shares held by him is noted. It must contain the following particulars:

a. the name of the company, with "Limited" as the last word of the name

b. its registered office

c. the company's business

d. a statement that the liability of its members is limited

e. the amount of share capital, the number of shares and their par value (for example, £100 capital divided into 100 shares of £1 each). No person signing the Memorandum may take less than one share. There are few restrictions on the classes of shares but voting rights must exist

f. other items such as classes of shares, directors, quorum, and other matters of importance.

The Memorandum is the constitution of the company and its legal framework. Great care is required in drafting the business objects of the company to ensure not only that they are sufficiently wide to cover the immediate trading proposals but also that they will allow for extending the company's activities.

It is also necessary to have Articles of Association which lay down how the company is to be run. These must also be signed by each original subscriber.

When the Memorandum and Articles of Association have been completed they are delivered together with certain registration forms and the necessary fees, to the Registrar of Companies. The Registrar will then issue a Certificate of Incorporation. At that point the company formally comes into legal existence. No further authority is necessary in the case of a private company.

A public company cannot commence business or enter into any contract, except provisionally, until the Registrar issues a Trading Certificate.

Public or Private Company

The decision to form either a public or a private company will depend upon particular requirements concerning the raising of capital and share control.

For private company status, which in itself carries certain privileges and obligations, a number of requirements must be fulfilled. In particular the Articles of Association of the company must:

    a. restrict the right to transfer shares

    b. limit the number of its members to no more than 50 (excluding employee and ex-employee shareholders)

    c. prohibit any invitation to the public to subscribe for shares or debentures.

Private companies need have only two shareholders and one director. They do not have to file an annual report but they must publish their financial statements.

Public companies must have at least seven shareholders and two directors. They must file annual reports.

The U.K. government is taking a hard look at the rules on "inside trading" and conflicts of interests on the part of company directors (executives).

At present there are no laws relating to public issues. The London Stock Exchange is a self-regulating body and it has a code for "take-over" and other situations.

Changes in capital require approval from shareholders. Various classes of shares are permitted. The rights of any particular class of shareholders may not be altered without the approval of 75% of those shareholders. Public companies must keep registers of their shares. English companies may not purchase their own shares.

Annual shareholders meetings must be held.

Company Registration Fees

Company registration fees are laid down in the Companies Act and, in the case of a company limited by shares, are based on the nominal capital.

Registration fees are £2 per £2,000 of stated capital plus a capital transfer tax of 0.5%. The minimum fee is about $100 for a minimum capital company. There is no law dictating the minimum capital for a company but there can be no no-par shares. Shares may not be issued for less than par.

Management

Company law is fairly permissive regarding management.

A company is managed by directors appointed by the shareholders. Directors can be removed by resolution and must retire at age 70. The directors appoint a managing director. Directors must not abuse their "insider" status in dealing with their company's shares. There are no restrictions on the nationality of directors. A company may be a director. There must also be a secretary.

148   Each company must keep a register of its directors and secretary

showing their names, addresses, nationalities and occupations.

Management must appoint independent auditors and prepare balance sheets, profit and loss statements and annual reports with recommendations for dividends and reserve allocations.

Limited Company or Branch Office

An overseas concern, whether or not incorporated, may trade in the U.K. either through its own personnel, agents or licensees. Any company, or individual, trading other than in its own name, has to register the name at the Business Names Registry Office.

An overseas company operating a branch office in the U.K. must do so in its own name. Within a month of setting up business it should file with the Registrar of Companies the following documents:

a. a certified copy and a certified English translation of the company's constitution

b. the names, addresses and occupations of the directors and secretary of the company

c. the name and address of at least one official, resident in the U.K., who is legally authorized to accept legal notices on behalf of the company.

In addition to the above requirements, the company must publish its name, country of incorporation, directors and their nationality on its letterheads.

Taxation in the U.K.
General

The tax laws in the U.K. have changed many times over the last few years. More changes are on the cards.

The system is very gentlemanly. No one has ever gone to jail for tax evasion in England.

Questions of residence and domicile are important and complex. Persons not domiciled in the U.K. can gain tax advantages although resident there.

The tax year starts on April 6. Annual tax assessments are based on the preceeding year's income.

Individuals

The basic rate of individual tax is 33%; there is then a sliding scale up to 78% at £10,000. There is a 15% surcharge on investment income over £2,000 and a surcharge on earned income in excess of £4,500. Deductions are allowed for children and adults.

Capital gains are taxed at 30%.

Employees and employers pay tax on a P.A.Y.E. system (pay as you earn). Both contribute to it.

A visitor to the U.K. is normally taxed as a resident if he remains six months or more in any tax year or stays over 90 days a year for a period of four consecutive years. A person who maintains a home in the U.K. is taxed as a resident, irrespective of the length of his visits, unless he works abroad full time.

A non-resident is taxable on income from services performed in the U.K. A person who is domiciled outside the U.K. but resident in the U.K. and who has a foreign employer, is exempt from tax on 50% of his earned income.

Company Taxation

Companies pay a 52% corporation profits tax. Companies may choose their own fiscal years. Corporation tax is paid on total profits. The company deducts 3/7ths (42.82%) from dividends. This is credited to the company's tax bill. Each shareholder can credit against his income tax the amount of corporation tax paid on his dividends. 3/7ths works out to 30% for the average taxpayer, so most of his tax is paid. U.S. shareholders can apply for tax relief, based on double tax treaty arrangements, to recapture half of the 3/7ths.

Companies pay tax on capital gains at slightly less than corporation tax rates.

Close companies (five or less shareholders) can be taxed heavily if they do not distribute what the Inland Revenue thinks is enough of their profits.

Accounting

British accounting standards are high and are the most similar to the U.S. standards of any country in the EEC.

Full reporting is the standard—not the law. U.K. chartered accountants are less inclined to bend the rules than their counterparts elsewhere.

Depreciation is flexible and 100% of capital equipment can be written off in the first year.

Double Taxation Agreements

The U.K. has double tax agreements with many overseas countries. Some classes of income are exempted from British taxation, even though arising in Britain, if they are received by a non-resident and are taxed in his own country. There are double taxation agreements with the U.S. and most European countries for the remittance of income and profits. Under the treaty with the U.S., withholding tax is limited to 15%.

Value-Added Tax

Value-added tax (VAT) was introduced on April 1, 1973, at the rate of

10% on the supply of goods and services in the U.K., and on imports, subject to certain exceptions.

There are a series of other taxes, including stamp tax (on property and other transfers, the rates are from 0.5% to 1%), customs and excise taxes, automobile taxes and estate taxes.

Local Taxation

Local taxes or "rates" are imposed to finance local authorities. These are based on the "rateable value" of land and building and are paid on the occupiers. Rates vary from one district to another.

Government Control
Trade

There is legislation to curb monopolistic and restrictive trade practices. Restrictive trading agreements must be registered with the Registrar of Restrictive Trading Agreements, who can ask the Restrictive Practices Court to declare them void.

Mergers which would lead to a monopoly situation (a 25% market share) or those which involve the acquisition of assets valued at more than £5 million fall within the scope of the Monopolies and Mergers Act of 1965.

A Panel has been set up by financial institutions to supervise a code of conduct for companies engaged in take-over or merger transactions.

Price Controls

Wage and price controls were introduced in 1973 to help curb inflation.

Import Controls

A Department of Trade and Industry license is needed for all goods imported into the U.K. But the extension of "Open General Licenses" to an ever increasing range of goods has freed the great majority of goods from control.

Virtually all imports into Britain are free from quota restrictions, although trade with a few countries is subject to special controls.

Export Controls

Apart from exchange control regulations, export controls are only imposed for specific reasons. These include the need to control scarce materials, to prevent the export of works of art and to control strategically important goods. The majority of goods subject to export control are in this last category, but curbs have been relaxed in recent years.

151

Raising Capital

The raising of capital by U.K. companies is not generally subject to Treasury control. Approval is needed for transactions on behalf of non-residents, involving a sum of more than £50,000 in any 12 months. Assent is normally given if the project will help strengthening the balance of payments position. The timing of all issues of capital of £1 million and over has to be arranged with the Bank of England.

The Stock Exchange

Outside of the U.S., the London Stock Exchange is the largest in the world. In addition to providing a market for existing securities, the Stock Exchange plays an important part in the provision of finance for new industries and the expansion of existing industries. The London Stock Exchange is a self-regulating organization. New issues are usually offered directly to the public through an intermediary institution, such as an issuing house. New issues may also be "placed"—that is, sold privately to a limited number of investors, or made available by the company to existing shareholders through "rights" issues.

Any company listed on the New York or American Stock Exchanges will automatically qualify for listing on the London Stock Exchange.

Insurance Companies

Insurance companies' funds are mainly invested in stock exchange securities, and the companies are active in underwriting or taking up new issues.

Business Incentives

Excellent incentives are offered to companies setting up in "development areas."

In addition to favorable tax features (100% depreciation of capital goods in the year of acquisition), there are grants up to 22% of the cost of plant and machinery for approved projects. Capital expenditures qualify for 100% "write off" allowances in the first year except for industrial buildings which qualify for 44% depreciation the first year and 4% per year after that.

There are special tax incentives for ship-building and total tax avoidance is possible.

Real Estate

Office rents in London are the highest in the world and can reach $100 or more per square foot although $60-30 is more usual.

Property values in Britain have risen at a staggering rate since 1945 and are very high by U.S. standards.

Building Societies
Banks do not generally deal in mortgages or lend money against real estate.

The 460 or so building societies are the main source of funds for house purchases. Long-term loans are made against a mortgage on the property. Loans are occasionally made on commercial, industrial or agricultural property, but societies are limited to individual advances of £13,000. The funds of building societies come mainly from the public who invest in their shares and place money on deposit. Depositors have preference in mortgage applications.

Labor
Britain's labor relations are bad. There is an Industrial Relations Act but it is not used.

British workers are poorly paid by Western standards.

There are few labor laws. Little notice is required for dismissal and there are no minimum wage or maximum work week rules, except for women and children. Two weeks vacation per year is standard.

Social security is elaborate. There is free medical care for all—even tourists. Everyone makes a contribution to the National Health Service by purchasing stamps each week.

Unemployment benefits and pensions are broad in their coverage.

Employers are required to take out insurance against liability for injury or disease sustained by their employees in the course of employment.

A non-British national employed in the U.K. usually needs a Department of Employment work permit. EEC nationals do not have this problem. The permit should be obtained by the employer before the employee arrives in the U.K.

Patents, Trademarks and Copyrights
Britain's law on patents (16 years) is fairly standard and the fees are low. Patents are valid for 16 years and should be registered at the Patent Registry Office.

Trademarks must also be registered at the Patent Office. They are valid for seven years and are renewable.

Copyrights are valid for a period of 50 years after the death of the author.

Gibraltar (The Rock)
Gibraltar occupies the rocky headland at the southern tip of Spain. It is a mere three miles long by 1,300 yards wide. The 30,000 inhabitants of The Rock speak English but are mainly of Portuguese, Maltese and Genoese descent. Britain captured The Rock in 1704 and has held it ever

153

since. However, Spain still claims sovereignty over it.

The Economy

The economy depends largely on tourism, the naval dockyard and other expenditures by Britain's armed forces. Spanish restrictions, which have increased in intensity since 1964, have halted the flow of labor, commercial traffic and imports from Spain.

As part of the Sterling Area Gibraltar is important to foreigners doing business in the U.K. and the EEC.

Currency

The Gibraltar pound is at par with the U.K. pound. British notes are not legal tender, but free circulation is allowed. There is no restriction on the amount of currency which may be taken into Gibraltar but the amount taken out must not exceed that declared on entry.

There are five banks operating in Gibraltar.

Taxation
On Income

Residents of Gibraltar pay tax on income, derived from, or received in Gibraltar; and, in the case of a company, on dividends and interest. Profits from a business carried on wholly outside Gibraltar are not subject to tax unless the profits are remitted to Gibraltar.

The highest rate of income tax for both individuals and companies is the standard rate of 30%. Reduced rates apply to the first £3,500 of an individual's income.

There is no tax on capital or wealth, and no capital gains tax.

Dividends and Interest

Withholding tax is not paid on the dividends of exempt companies (see below) and shipping companies. Any other company resident in Gibraltar must deduct tax at the standard rate when paying dividends and annual interest. Interest on bank accounts held in Gibraltar by non-residents and exempt companies is not subject to tax.

The remittance system for personal income tax liability in Gibraltar is similar to that in the U.K.

Although Gibraltar's tax laws do not contain any specific provisions exempting certain trusts from income tax, in practice no tax liability arises in cases where no beneficial interest accrues to person, ordinarily resident in Gibraltar.

Forms of Doing Business

(See the section on Britain).

Gibraltar became firmly established as a tax haven with the passing of the Companies (Taxation and Concessions) Ordinance. It grants income tax and estate duty concessions to companies incorporated in Gibraltar and registered as exempt. An exempt company can engage in virtually any type of activity or business which does not involve any person or company ordinarily resident in Gibraltar (other than another exempt company). No Gibraltarians, or residents of Gibraltar, may hold any beneficial interest in the shares of an exempt company. They may nevertheless hold such shares as nominees with the permission of the Financial Secretary, who is bound to absolute secrecy on the ownership of the shares.

An exemption certificate grants full freedom from Gibraltar income tax and estate duty and is valid for 25 years.

Introduction

The main Channel Islands are Jersey, Guernsey, Alderney and Sark. While not members of the Common Market, they do have a special relationship with the EEC. They are also part of the Sterling Area.

Currency

The currency is the same as Britain's.

The islands' financial communities were given a new spurt in June, 1972, when the Sterling Area was contracted, leaving the Channel Islands prominent among the very small number of "tax havens" left within the new Sterling Area. The immediate result was that a number of banks asked permission to open offices there.

A number of mutual fund operators also moved into the islands at that time.

The Channel Islands and the EEC

The Channel Islands have a special relationship with the Common Market. They are not "in association" in the strict sense that term has for some countries. They have completely free trade *without value-added tax* (which would have been an intolerable burden for a community so reliant upon imports). They are committed to: (1) the gradual harmonization of their customs and excise systems with those of the Community; and, (2) the revision of their legislation so that there will be no discrimination between Continental nationals and U.K. nationals wishing to work or stay in the islands.

Of course, the Islands remain free to discriminate against all nationals equally. Jersey does so with its "rich settlers" rules which require new residents to pay minimum annual taxes of about $10,000. The rules were introduced to stem the flow of Britons seeking the advantages of a tax haven so close to home.

So far the Continental members of the EEC have not shown much

155

interest in the Channel Islands. This is probably because few Continentals actually know where the Channel Islands are, and even fewer understand their new arrangements.

The Channel Islands have an interesting range of fiscal benefits to offer. Low taxation, the absence of death duties, together with good government and political stability, make them unusually attractive to overseas corporate establishments and wealthy individuals.

Financial Aspects, of Channel Islands as Tax Haven

Financial organizations handling offshore money have grown apace during the past few years. A reasonable estimate is that some $2,000 million is on deposit through investment banks, savings banks and clearing banks. Nearly all this money is actually placed in the London money market, giving rise to the charge that Channel Island institutions are simply acting as "post offices" and that the real profits are being made in London.

A "turn" of a fraction of 1% is earned on the funds that pass through. It is estimated that Jersey's income from these financial operations is about $3 million a year—some 10% of the islands' annual income. Indirect benefits are many. Travel to and from the islands is stimulated all year round. Local jobs are created for office workers.

Jersey

Jersey is the largest of the Channel Islands. It lies in the English Channel, about 14 miles west of the Cherbourg Peninsula.

The island is approximately 10 miles long and 6 miles wide. The total population is about 75,000. Nearly half live in the capital, St. Helier, which is the port and principal trading center of the island.

Government

Jersey's governmental connection with the U.K. devolves primarily from the Crown and not from the British government. While in strict law the U.K. Parliament can legislate for Jersey in all matters, this has now been limited by usage. In tax and domestic matters, the island is self-governing. The U.K. is responsible for Jersey's external relations.

Business Entities in Jersey

a. Jersey registered companies.
b. Jersey registered companies controlled outside Jersey.
c. Partnerships.
d. Discretionary fund trusts.

Jersey Registered Companies

156   Companies registered in Jersey may only be formed with limited

liability. There is no distinction between public and private companies. It is possible for a Jersey company to be quoted on a recognized stock exchange. Formation of a Jersey company costs approximately $500.

All companies are liable to income tax on profits at the standard rate of 20% *on income earned in Jersey*.

Trading companies may be formed to trade within the island or to handle external trading transactions. In the latter case, an "external" company is preferred with its capital expressed in a currency other than sterling.

Companies registered in Jersey, but doing business outside the island pay no tax on profits and only $750 per year "franchise" tax. Many companies are therefore formed in Jersey and have their main offices in Sark (another Channel Island) or another country.

Investment holding companies are those holding investments for the purpose of earning income. If profits on the sale of investments are incidental to the company's main purpose, they will not be subject to Jersey income tax.

Investment dealing companies pay income tax on both trading profits and investment income. Residents of foreign countries can normally form an investment holding or trading company without difficulty.

Company Formation

Formation of a Jersey company usually takes between three weeks and a month. However, this could take longer if the company has unusual rules or needs exchange control permission.

Jersey limited liability companies have to be registered in the Royal Court of Jersey. If the Memorandum and Articles of Association do not limit trading; and neither the Jersey Treasury nor the Bank of England have placed restrictions on its activities, the company is free to trade as it wishes. There are no restrictions covering nationality or residence of directors or shareholders.

A company must have three founder members each subscribing for a minimum of three shares at a par value. A Jersey company must have a registered office in Jersey and must have its full name above its offices and on its stationery.

The Memorandum and Articles of Association of Jersey registered companies should include provision for the company to invest outside Jersey. Companies without this provision (or bailiff's clause) cannot invest elsewhere.

Guernsey

Guernsey is the second largest of the Channel Islands. Compared to Jersey, Guernsey like Alderney and Sark is of minor importance as a

157

financial center.

The laws and taxes are similar to Jersey.

Under Guernsey laws, companies are classified into two broad categories—holding companies and trading companies.

The term holding company has not been legally defined but generally includes those companies holding portfolios of other companies.

Guernsey law states that a company must have a minimum of two directors and a maximum of five. All the directors may be residents of the Channel Islands. Directors may appoint alternates to act for them.

General Points on Channel Island Tax Law

There are no net-worth taxes in Guernsey and Jersey.

There are no stamp duties on patent royalties, dividends, and interest paid to either residents or non-residents.

There are no stamp duties on share certificates, bearer bonds, or transfer of securities.

Withholding taxes are not paid on dividends from Channel Island companies which are not controlled in Guernsey or Jersey (i.e. non-residents for tax purposes).

Interest paid by non-resident companies from non-resident sources of income is not liable to local taxation.

Interest paid by banks is not subject to withholding tax.

Isle of Man

The Isle of Man is situated in the Irish Sea. It is one of the British Isles but does not form part of the United Kingdom. It has an area of 227 miles and a population of about 50,000.

The Manx Parliament, founded in 930 A.D., is "The House of Keys", a translation of which from the Norse language means "The Chaser". The members are elected by the residents of the island where party politics are minimal.

The currency is on par with English money and the same exchange control regulations prevail.

The volume of business activity is very low.

It has separate tax laws with very attractive tax rates. Company formation and tax regulations for non-resident companies are roughly similar to those of the Channel Islands.

Company tax is $21\frac{1}{2}\%$ on local income, and nil on income earned abroad if the main office of the company is not in the Isle of Man.

X IRELAND

Ireland

ÉIRE

1   2   3
1 green
2 white
3 orange

Total population 2,987,248

Area 27,136 sq ms / 70,282 sq kms

Population density 108 per sq m / 42 per sq km

Form of government Parliamentary democracy. Executive power is vested in the Government under the Taoiseach (Prime Minister). Legislative power is exercised by the Oireachtas (Parliament), consisting of the President, the Dáil Eireann (House of Representatives), and the Seanad Eireann (Senate). Election to the Oireachtas is by proportional representation based on universal suffrage.

Head of state The President/elected for 7 years by direct plebiscite

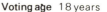

Voting age 18 years

Public health Free or subsidized health service depending on income.
3,011 doctors (1966)
59,091 hospital beds (1966)

Major imports Raw materials, machinery, foodstuffs, chemicals, transport equipment

Major exports Live animals, meat products, textiles, foodstuffs, drink

Belfast

Dublin

|0|50|100|150m|
|0|100|200 km|

Mercantile marine 72 vessels

Military personnel 10,000

Official language(s) Irish, English

School-leaving age 15 years

Higher education 2
universities/19,700 places

Currency Irish pound

Membership of international
organisations OECD, Council of
Europe, EEC, the UN and its
agencies

E is for Ireland

Eire (The Republic of Ireland) is part of the island known as Ireland.
Since 1920, the island has been partitioned between the Republic of
Ireland and Northern Ireland (Ulster). Northern Ireland is part of the
United Kingdom and consists of the six north-eastern counties of the
island. The remaining 26 counties form the Irish Republic.
Eire is 27,000 square miles.
There are about 3 million people in Ireland.

Agriculture

Agriculture is Ireland's principal industry, employing 27% of the
working population. It accounts for one-sixth of the national income and
for about 42% of total exports.

Irish agriculture has benefited substantially from high prices for its
good quality cattle and beef.

Industry

Over the past 20 years industrial employment has risen by 41%, and
the value of industrial exports has increased five-fold in the past decade.
Industry in general is expected to expand substantially under the
stimulus of EEC membership, though certain industries, unable to
compete in circumstances of free trade will contract.

Ireland has large deposits of lead and zinc and is exploring the Irish
Sea for oil and gas.

EEC Membership

The Republic became a full member of the EEC on January 1, 1973
on terms similar to those governing the admission of the U.K.
and Denmark.

A special protocol agreed between Ireland and the EEC is attached to
Ireland's treaty of accession. This protocol acknowledges Ireland as a
developing region and allows for the continuation of its range of
incentives to promote industrial development (see section on
investment incentives).

The principal terms of this protocol are:

1. Ireland will honor incentives already promised to new firms

162

manufacturing for export.

2. The present range of incentives will apply until the EEC's state aid program is revised.

3. If modifications to Ireland's incentives become necessary, revised incentives will be offered which will be equally effective in promoting industrial development in Ireland.

Special arrangements were also made to permit the Republic to import certain raw materials free of tariffs; to continue to protect the automotive assembly industry until 1985; to maintain quantitative restrictions on industrial imports until 1975, and on certain textiles and clothing from low-cost countries until 1979. In cases of extreme urgency the Republic may, until 1977, take defensive "anti-dumping" measures.

The Anglo-Irish Free Trade Agreement

The "Anglo-Irish Free Trade Area Agreement", which provides a time-table for the elimination of duty on industrial goods of U.K. origin, continues to apply. Therefore until mid-1977 (when all EEC trade barriers will be gone), U.K. exporters will enjoy certain tariff advantages in Ireland over other members of the Common Market.

This agreement gives assurances on the export of Irish agricultural products into Britain and will remove protective duties in 10 equal annual stages.

General

Ireland's native tongue is Gaelic but English is spoken everywhere and literacy is high.

Ireland uses feet, miles and pounds but will change to the metric system.

Ireland has many attractions for the investor. It has a temperate, marine climate and a good location (close to the U.S.). There are fine air and sea ports, waterways, road and rail networks, together with a complete range of ancilliary services and good communication facilities.

The U.S. enjoys a favorable balance of trade with Ireland and is its main trading partner after neighbouring Britain.

About 125 U.S. manufacturing enterprises were established in Ireland between 1960 and 1972. This represents 26% of all foreign investment in Ireland. Because of the favorable tax situation in Ireland, American companies find they can have access to Britain and the rest of the Common Market and realize higher net profits than if they located elsewhere.

Britain is the only country which invests more in Ireland than the U.S.

Political Structure

Ireland is a parliamentary democracy.   163

After hundreds of years of struggle with the English, the Irish Free State was established in the 1920s as part of the British Commonwealth. Ireland left the Commonwealth and became a republic in 1948.

The "troubles" over the division of Ireland into the Republic in the South and Ulster in the North continue to affect policies and relations between the U.K. and Eire.

The Irish Parliament (the Oireachtes) consists of two houses— a House of Representatives (Dail Eireann) and a Senate (Seanad Eireann). It has an elected President who is Head of State and a Prime Minister (Taoiseach) who is Head of Government.

Elections for both houses are held at least every five years. The Dail has legislative power. The Seanad consists of Government nominees and representatives of various vocational and cultural interests including the universities. Its powers are limited.

The government departments responsible for trade and economic affairs are the Department of Finance and the Department of Industry and Commerce.

Legal System

The administration of justice in Ireland resembles closely the common law system developed in England. (See chapter on Britain.) The system includes a Supreme Court with final and conclusive jurisdiction. Judges are fully independent.

General Business Pointers
Hours of Business

Business hours are usually 09:30–17:30. However, banks are open from 10:00–12:30 and from 13:30–15:00. Banks usually stay open until 17:00 one night per week.

Vacations
New Year's Day
St. Patrick's Day (March 17)
Good Friday
Easter Monday
1st Monday in June
1st Monday in August
Christmas Day
Boxing Day

Currency and Banking

The monetary unit is the Irish pound and it is maintained at parity with the British pound sterling. Irish currency denominations are identical to those of sterling. (See chapter on Britain.) The Central Bank of Ireland is responsible for issuing currency and administering exchange control regulations.

Banking in Ireland is under a great deal of foreign influence. Two of the four "Irish" banks are controlled by Midland Bank and National Westminster Bank of England. In addition American banks (U.S. and Canada) control 20% of total bank deposits in Ireland.

Exchange Control

Exchange control regulations in Ireland parallel those in force in the U.K. As the Republic is a member of the Sterling Area, there are no restrictions on investment in Ireland by a U.K. resident. The "Sterling Area" now consists only of the U.K., the Channel Islands, the Isle of Man, Gibraltar and the Republic of Ireland. The remainder of the former "Scheduled Territories" is now generally known as the "Overseas Sterling Area".

Investments by Non-Residents of the Sterling Area

The regulations on investments in Ireland by non-residents of the Sterling Area are as follows:

a. Central Bank permission is needed to purchase shares in unquoted companies. Permission is normally granted provided the funds originate outside the British Isles.

b. Permission is not needed to buy shares quoted on an Irish stock exchange provided the funds come from outside the Sterling Area.

c. Loans from non-sterling sources may be used rather than investment capital, provided Central Bank permission is obtained. Companies controlled by non-residents may not borrow from Irish banks without Central Bank approval. Where the purpose of the borrowing is to finance capital needs, this approval is normally given.

Irish residents and companies seeking to invest abroad face restrictions similar to those imposed by the Bank of England on U.K. residents.

Repatriation of Foreign Investments

a. Approval for unquoted companies to issue shares to, and borrow from, non-residents carries with it the right to repay loans and to repatriate the capital.

b. Similar rules apply where the original investment was in an Irish branch of a non-resident company.

c. Loans made from external sources with Central Bank approval may be repaid out of the cash flow.

d. The transfer abroad of dividends paid by subsidiaries and the profits of branches is permitted; so is interest paid on loans from the parent company. This interest must be similar to prevailing local rates.   165 *e.* Permission is given freely for the remittance of royalties (provided the relative agreements were registered with and approved by the Central Bank) and for the transfer of funds to pay for services and technical assistance rendered abroad.

f. When quoted securities are sold the proceeds can be freely transferred abroad. The same applies to dividends from quoted securities.

Imports and Exports

Exchange control permission is not needed to order goods from outside the Sterling Area, provided the goods are to be used in Ireland, are to be delivered within nine months of the order, and are to be paid for in foreign currency or "external" currency. Where the total value of imported goods exceeds £2,000, a formal application for permission to pay must be submitted to a bank. If the value does not exceed £2,000, then it is only necessary to satisfy a bank that the transaction is genuine by providing evidence, such as an invoice or contract.

In general, exports over £100 to places outside the Sterling Area must be paid for in a specified foreign currency or external sterling.

External Accounts

A person who moves to Ireland from outside the Sterling Area with the intention of staying there for up to one year is non-resident. His bank account is designated an "external account". External accounts are not subject to exchange control regulations and are freely convertible into any other currency. Permission is needed to make payments from a resident account to an external account because it is equivalent to transferring funds outside the Sterling Area.

Foreign Nationals' Funds

Personnel from outside the Sterling Area assigned to an Irish subsidiary or branch for a temporary, although indefinite period will normally be regarded as temporarily resident for exchange control purposes. They may remit up to 50% of their earnings to their home countries. In cases where such foreign personnel intend to live in Ireland for at least three years, they will be regarded as Irish residents for exchange control purposes.

Rules applicable to foreign-owned businesses
Prohibited Activities

Subject to exchange control approval, which is rarely refused, foreign firms are free to carry on business in Ireland either by forming a new company, a branch or by the acquisition of an established Irish company.

Exceptions to this are as follows:

a. Industrial enterprises—the production of sugar and electricity by foreign firms is not permitted.

b. Non-industrial enterprises—foreign firms or persons cannot enter the insurance business. All companies wanting to enter these activities must be controlled by Irish citizens. Foreigners may not establish businesses in air or rail transport.

c. Real estate—there are no restrictions on the purchase of real estate of any kind in cities and larger towns. Land Commission consent is needed for the purchase of real estate outside urban areas unless the purchaser:

   i. is an Irish citizen, or

   ii. has been resident in Ireland continuously for seven years, or

   iii. has a certificate from the Department of Industry and Commerce showing that the real estate is being bought for industrial purposes and not agriculture, or

   iv. the real estate is for private residential purposes and does not exceed five acres.

Foreigners can get permission to purchase a farm in certain circumstances (e.g. if the property is a stud farm).

Forms of Doing Business

A business may be carried out in Ireland by:

1. Two or more individuals in partnership.
2. A company incorporated under the Companies Act 1963.
3. A branch of a foreign company.
4. An individual on his own.

Partnership

A partnership is an association of persons carrying on a business in common. The number of partners must not exceed 20 (or 10 in the case of a bank). The liability of general partners is unlimited and extends to all their private assets.

In Irish law a partnership has no separate legal status and is not required to publish its accounts.

Partners may trade under any name provided the name is not calculated to deceive or to cause confusion with the name of other businesses.

The Registration of Business Names Act, 1963 requires registration of a name when the partnership name does not consist of the surnames of all the partners. This also applies to an individual who does business under a name other than his own. It is a simple formality.

Companies

An Irish company can be created quickly and comparatively cheaply. 167

There are three types of Irish companies:

1. *Companies limited by shares*—similar to a U.S. corporation. The liability of the shareholders is limited to the unpaid amount, if any, of the full issue price of their shares.

2. *Companies limited by guaranty*—limit the liability of the members to the amount which they agree to contribute to the assets of the company in the event of liquidation—generally £1 to £5 each.

A limited guaranty company may have shares. Then the members have the double liability of having to pay the issue price of their shares and to honor their guarantees in the event of liquidation.

3. *Unlimited companies*—whose members are liable to the last penny of their fortunes if the company becomes insolvent.

Guaranty companies and unlimited companies are seldom used for trading purposes.

Formation

The Companies Act 1963 provides a simple and inexpensive method of forming companies. It follows the British system.

The Memorandum and Articles of Association are lodged with the Registrar of Companies together with a declaration that all the requirements of the Companies Act 1963 have been complied with and a statement of the initial capital of the company.

The Company is formed when the Registrar of Companies issues a Certificate of Incorporation.

Capital duty, a registration fee and some small filing fees have to be paid to the Registrar. Capital duty is calculated at a rate of 1/4% on the value of the issued share capital of the company.

The registration fee runs from £2 where the capital is £100 to £28.75 where capital is £100,000. It increases by 25p. for each £1,000 in excess of £100,000.

Public and Private Companies (See chapter on Britain)

A *public company* is any limited liability company other than a private company. It must have a minimum of seven members. Before it can trade it must file a prospectus (or its equivalent), it must obtain a certificate entitling it to trade and must raise all its initial capital requirements in its first public offering. These requirements combined with the Irish desire for secrecy indicate why there are not many public companies in Ireland. It is better to form a private company and convert it to a public company when the need arises.

Within 60 days of the annual general meeting, public companies must file a certified copy of their accounts with the Registrar of Companies in Dublin.

Accounting practices are the same as in Britain.

There are over 40,000 *private companies* in Ireland.

A private company has the following features:

i. There must be a minimum of two members.

ii. It can be formed more simply than a public company and therefore more cheaply.

iii. It can commence business immediately on incorporation whereas a public company has to comply with a number of formalities.

iv. It will not have to disclose much information about its affairs, nor will it have to publish its annual accounts.

v. Membership must be limited to a maximum of 50 (excluding employees and ex-employees who become members while employed).

vi. Restrictions must be imposed on the right to transfer shares.

vii. It is prohibited from inviting the public to subscribe for its shares or debentures.

Special features of Irish companies

a. The identity of shareholders need not be disclosed as shares can be held in the names of nominees.

b. In the case of a private company, a minimum paid up share capital is not needed.

c. Loan raising is greatly facilitated by the ability of companies to create the type of security known as a "floating charge" (a flexible loan against the company's assets whose value may vary with market conditions).

d. Shares may be issued with no voting rights, multiple voting rights or limited voting rights, and with rights to participate in assets on liquidation. A register of shareholders must be maintained.

Company letterheads must carry the name and nationality of the directors. A foreign company must show its nationality and whether the liability of its members is limited.

Status of Foreign Companies

The status of a foreign-owned company or branch is exactly the same as that of an Irish-owned enterprise. There are no requirements for capital investment or directors. There are no restrictions on the location of foreign-owned companies, although the choice of location may affect state aid. No difficulty is experienced in obtaining work permits for foreign management and technical personnel. Permits are not required for persons born in the U.K.

Taxation
Personal Taxes

There are two types of personal taxes:

a. Income Tax.   169 *b.* Surtax.

Income Tax—This is levied at 35% of income after certain allowances. Tax on salaries and pensions is collected under a P.A.Y.E. (Pay-as-you-earn) scheme under which the appropriate tax is withheld on payment.

A partnership is not taxed as a separate entity—the profits are allocated to and the tax levied on the individual partners.

Principal allowances:

1. Earned income allowance—25% of earned income. (Maximum £500.)
2. Personal allowances—single person £299; widow or widower—£324.
3. Child allowance—varies on age from £132 to £170 per child.
4. Allowances are also made on insurance premiums, bank interest, dependent relatives, etc.

Surtax—This is additional to income tax and is levied on earned income in excess of £5,000 or unearned income in excess of £3,000 at the following rates:

First £2,000 of excess income—15%

Next £2,000 of excess income—30%

Balance of excess income—45%

Individuals resident in Ireland, but not domiciled there, are liable to Irish income tax and surtax on income arising in Ireland or the U.K. Income from abroad is liable only to the extent it is remitted to Ireland (as is the case in Britain).

Company Taxation

There are two types of company taxes:

a. Income Tax.

b. Corporation Profits Tax.

Income Tax—This is levied at a flat 35% on profits. Companies not managed and controlled in Ireland are taxed only on profits made in Ireland, subject to double taxation agreements.

Unlike the U.S., tax is withheld at source on dividends. However, high income individuals may later be subject to surtax.

Corporation Profits Tax—This is additional to income tax and is payable by companies at the following rates:

$7\frac{1}{2}$% on first £2,500 of profits.

23% on profits over £2,500.

Companies incorporated in Ireland are liable for tax on all their profits. In calculating income tax, corporation tax is allowed as a deduction.

Taken together, the combined effect of income tax and corporation tax produces a total tax rate which rises from around 40% on small profits to some 50% for larger profits.

Determination of Profits

There is no general definition of profits or income. They are usually determined by the normal principles of commercial accountancy.

For expenditure to be deductible it must be:

a. Non-capital

b. Wholly and exclusively laid out for the purposes of the trade

Losses may be carried forward indefinitely until absorbed by future profits.

Depreciation

On calculating profits for income tax and corporation tax, deductions are allowed for depreciation of fixed assets as follows:

1. *Plant and Machinery*

a. Annual allowances may be claimed for new and used plant and machinery. These vary with type and estimated useful life from 10%–25%.

b. Free depreciation; the annual allowances described above may be increased up to 100% for new plant and machinery (other than road vehicles) used in designated areas (mainly the western part of the country).

c. Where free depreciation is not claimed, an initial allowance of 60% may be deducted for capital expenditures.

d. Balancing allowances and balancing charges are used to adjust any excess or deficiency in the allowances arising when plant and machinery cease to be used in the business.

2. *Industrial Buildings*

a. An initial allowance of 20% may be claimed for capital expenditures on the construction of an industrial building or on the provision of recreational facilities for employees.

b. An annual rate of 2% may be deducted for buildings which qualify for the initial allowance.

c. Balancing allowances and balancing charges are used to adjust any deficiency or excess in the allowances when an industrial building is sold.

3. *Hotels*

The initial allowance and the annual write-off rate is 10%.

Local Taxes

An annual tax known as "rates" is charged on property. It is a charge on land and buildings and is based on an artificial rental value of property. It works out at between 0.125% and 0.5% of the cost of land and buildings excluding the cost of machinery and plant. Firms may offset rates against profits for tax purposes.

Value-added tax was introduced in 1972. Most items are either charged 6.75% (necessities) or 19.5% (the basic rate) but luxury items

171

are charged much higher rates (36.75%).

Some General Points

There is no capital gains tax in Ireland.

Stamp duty is charged on the transfer of shares at the rate of 1% and on transfer of real property at rates from 2%–10%.

The Irish government has withdrawn the 20-year tax exemption on mining companies' profits. The tax exemption was introduced in 1967 to persuade international companies to finance mineral exploration in Ireland. It was instrumental in attracting some 90 companies to Ireland.

Investment Incentives

In its drive to attract new investment the Irish government offers attractive financial and other incentives.

These incentives according to the EEC Commission "go further than those of any other country in Europe in encouraging export industries and in attracting private capital for this purpose".

They are administered by a number of state-sponsored bodies who have been given responsibility for the promotion of industrial development in Ireland.

The principal organizations involved are:

1. The Industrial Development Authority (IDA)
   Lansdowne House,
   Ballsbridge
   Dublin 4

This organization has national responsibility for industrial development.

The Small Industries Division of IDA provides advisory and financial services to viable small-scale enterprises and helps in the establishment of new firms. Firms assisted under this program normally have a fixed asset investment of less than £100,000 and employ less than 50 people.

2. Shannon Free Airport Development Co. Ltd. (SFADCO)
   Shannon
   County Clare.

This organization has special responsibility for development of the Mid-West Region (counties Clare, Limerick and North Tipperary).

3. Gaeltarra Eireann
   North Forbache
   County Galway.

This organization has special responsibility for development of industries in Irish-speaking areas particularly in the northwest, west and southwest of the country.

4. *Irish Tourist Board* (Bord Faille Eireann)

This is the state-sponsored agency responsible for the development and promotion of tourism with particular emphasis on the hotel industry.

5. *Irish Export Board* (Coras Trachtala Teoranta)

This is the state organization for the promotion of exports. Its services to exporters cover a wide field. They include general information on shipping, export procedures and techniques, market research and assistance in arranging export marketing programs, trade fairs, etc. Incentive grants are provided for market research, trade fair participation and improved designs, etc.

6. *The Institute for Industrial Research and Standards*

This is a state-sponsored organization engaged in promoting scientific inquiry and improving industrial techniques. It carries out research and development projects on its own behalf but much of its work is concerned with projects undertaken at the request of industry. Its extensive facilities for materials testing, assessment of product quality and pollution control are available to all manufacturers in Ireland.

Summary of Main Incentives

1. *Complete tax exemption for* 15 *years* on profits generated by exports and partial exemption for the remaining years up to 1990. The granting of this relief is viewed by the state as a "contractual obligation".

The exemption applies on a pro-rata basis if all profits are not attributable to export sales. If total sales are £100,000 in a particular year and £50,000 is attributable to exports, then 50% of the company's profits are tax exempt.

Export tax relief is available to companies whose activities will improve Ireland's balance of payments. It relates only to companies and to "manufactured" goods. A broad view is taken of the definition of manufacturing.

At Shannon Free Port, complete tax exemption applies until 1990 and is available for warehousing and office projects as well as manufacturing projects.

2. *There are no restrictions on the repatriation of profits,* capital gains, or on proceeds from the sale or liquidation of any investment.

3. *Non-repayable cash grants* are made towards the cost of fixed assets (sites, site-development, buildings, new machinery and equipment). The grants are available up to a maximum of 50% in "designated areas" (mostly in the western half of the country) and 35% in the other areas.

Industrial development in the Dublin area is not encouraged.

In Gaelic-speaking areas grants up to 66% are available on the cost of factories, machinery and equipment. "Gaeltarra Eireann" may also provide equity participations ranging from 26% to 49%.

4. *Training and research and development grants*—The Industrial

173

Training Authority is responsible for training at all levels of industry and commerce. This body operates training centers at Dublin, Cork, Galway, Waterford, Shannon and Gweedore. More centers are planned.

The IDA has established an Industrial Research Park at Naas (20 miles from Dublin) to enable firms to carry out research and development at low cost.

5. *Guarantees of loans* and the subsidizing of interest on loans.

6. *Ready-made facilities* include advance factories and industrial services on industrial estates.

State-sponsored estates have been established at Galway, Waterford, Shannon, and Limerick while others, sponsored by private enterprise and local development authorities, have been set up in many other centers. Suitable housing for key workers is available close to the estates.

7. *Grants to service rent* on factories on the industrial estates.

8. *An "aftercare" service for newly established industries* in the early years of production.

9. *The services of several other state and private organizations* are also available to assist industrialists.

Stock Market

The Irish Stock Exchange is located in Dublin. Its rules are similar to the London Stock Exchange. A public issue should have a value of £250,000 representing at least 35% of the issued shares of the company. There are rigid rules for full disclosure in a prospectus.

Real Estate

See section on "Exchange Control—Prohibited Activities".

Labor

Ireland is short of skilled workers. Wages are low but rising rapidly. Social security insurance is compulsory for low wage earners. Both employer and employee contribute to it.

The maximum work week is 48 hours, but the average is 40 hours. Two weeks vacation with pay is compulsory after a year's employment.

Labor relations in Ireland are not very good. Unions are organized on an industry-wide basis although there are many craft unions.

Foreigners must have work and residence permits. Work permits are obtained from the Ministry of Labor. EEC nationals are subject to these rules until January 1, 1978.

Patents, Trademarks and Copyrights

Patents are granted for 16 years by the Controller of Industrial Property. Small renewal fees are payable annually after the fourth year.

174   Trademarks and copyrights follow the British system.

XI ITALY

Italy

REPUBBLICA ITALIANA

1 2 3
1 green
2 white
3 red

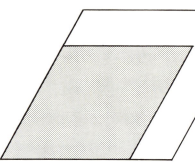

Total population 54,683,136

Area 116,280 sq ms/301,225 sq kms

Population density 470 per sq m/182 per sq km

 Form of government Democratic republic. Executive power is exercised by the government under a Prime Minister. Legislative power is vested in the Parliament comprising the Senate and the Chamber of Deputies. The Senate has 315 members elected on a proportional, regional basis. The Chamber of Deputies comprises 630 members elected for 5 years by direct, proportional, and universal suffrage.

 Head of state The President/elected by the Parliament for a single 7-year term

 Voting age 21 years

 Major imports Coal, timber, petroleum, meat, metals, mechanical and electrical equipment.

Major exports Foodstuffs, petroleum products, motor vehicles, clothing, plastics

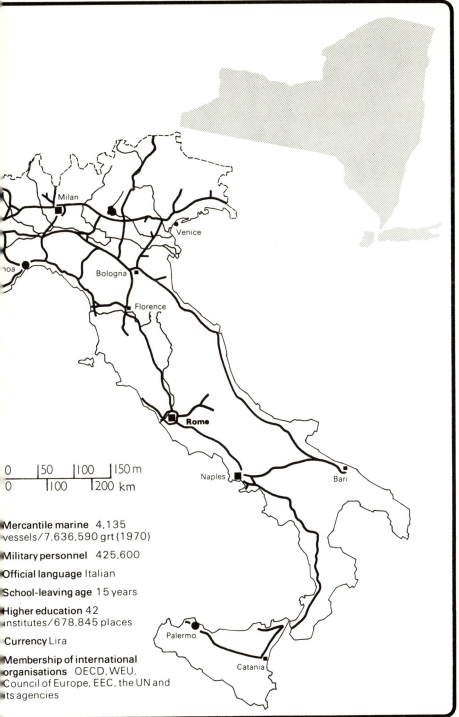

Milan

Venice

noa

Bologna

Florence

Rome

0 |50 |100 |150 m
0 |100 |200 km

Naples

Bari

Mercantile marine 4,135
vessels / 7,636,590 grt (1970)

Military personnel 425,600

Official language Italian

School-leaving age 15 years

Higher education 42
institutes / 678,845 places

Currency Lira

**Membership of international
organisations** OECD, WEU,
Council of Europe, EEC, the UN and
its agencies

Palermo

Catania

© DIAGRAM

When in Rome do be careful

Italy, a mountainous peninsula, shaped like a boot is probably the most beautiful and most disorganized member of the Common Market.

Every part of Italy has different scenery and each part is lovelier than the next. Small wonder that tourism is among its leading industries.

It has an area of 116,280 square miles, making it the second largest country in the EEC. Its population is about 55 million. The islands of Sicily and Sardinia are also part of Italy. To the north the Alps make a natural frontier with France, Switzerland, Austria and Yugoslavia. They enclose the great plain of northern Italy where the main industrial cities of Turin and Milan are situated. Milan (population 2 million) is the country's commercial and industrial capital.

Its true capital Rome (population 3 million) is in the central part of the country on the River Tiber. It is a city filled with ancient history.

In the south is Sicily, warm, fertile but economically backward.

While much economic effort has been expended, little progress has taken place in the south since the government's development program for the region was begun in 1950. The northern Italians look down upon their southern brothers.

Some 22% of Italy's commercial and banking services and 30% of its industry are in Lombardy, the area around Milan. Here, too, the market for consumer goods greatly exceeds that of any other comparable area in Italy. Lombardy's population is growing fast, and enjoys a "per capita" income considerably above the national average. The whole gamut of Italian industry is there.

Turin, in the northwest (population over 1 million), is the headquarters of Fiat, Europe's largest manufacturer of motor cars, and Italy's largest company. Turin's factories produce 75% of Italy's motor vehicles and over 80% of its roller bearings. Turin is also Italy's second largest steel-producing city.

Italy's largest port is Genoa on the west coast. Italy has a history of naval prowess. Venice on the east coast ruled much of the world in the Middle Ages.

Communications are good but the language is definitely Italian with
French as runner up.

Political Structure

Italy's lack of cohesion stems from the fact that it has existed as a unified state for only a century. Strong regional differences remain in social outlook and in commercial practice.

Italy has been a republic since World War II. The republic is decentralized, for administrative purposes, into 20 regions, 94 provinces and some 8,000 communes.

The central legislature consists of the Chamber of Deputies and the Senate. The members of both houses are elected by popular vote (one Deputy for every 80,000 inhabitants and one Senator for every 200,000). Legislation can be initiated in either house, but must be approved by a majority in each.

The Italian President is elected for a term of seven years by both houses in joint session. He nominates the Prime Minister who selects the cabinet. The Prime Minister, with his cabinet, determines policy. He must retain the confidence of Parliament when submitting and carrying out his legislative programs or the government will fall. The multiplicity of small parties often makes the formation of a government difficult. Italy has the largest Communist party in Western Europe.

Legal System

The Constitution is the principal law of the land.

The judiciary is independent of the government. The Constitutional Court decides all constitutional questions as well as disputes between the State and the regions. The Court of Cassation considers appeals from the lower courts.

Since litigation in Italy is a precarious and time consuming business— with delays of more than 10 years in certain cases—we will not dwell on Italian courts. Suffice it to say that there are Magistrates Courts, handling minor matters; Courts of Conciliation with higher jurisdiction; and Civil and Penal Tribunals with appellate authority under the Court of Cassation.

Stay out of the courts in Italy.

General Business Pointers

Except for marble, Italy is poor in raw materials. Exploration for oil is being carried out around Sicily.

Italy is the world's largest producer of small automobiles and of wine.

Its balance of payments has been very bad and looks like it is staying that way.

The U.S. is Italy's third largest trading partner and her No. 1 investor.

Shipping, aviation, newspapers, insurance, banking and pharmacies are restricted activities for foreigners.

Italy is on the metric system.

179

Newspapers, television and radio are well serviced. An English language paper, "The Daily American", is published in Rome.

Public Vacations

Italy has more vacations than any other Common Market country.
New Year's Day
Epiphany
Saint Joseph
Easter Monday
Anniversary of Liberation (April 25)
Labor Day (May 1)
Ascension Day
Anniversary of the Proclamation of the Republic (June 22)
Corpus Domini
Saints Peter and Paul
Assumption of the Blessed Virgin Mary
All Saints' Day
Anniversary of the Blessed Virgin Mary (November 4)
Immaculate Conception of the Blessed Virgin Mary (December 8)
Christmas Day
Saint Stephen's Day

Public offices are closed on the afternoons of August 14, November 2, Christmas Eve and New Year's Eve. August 15 is a bank holiday. Business is disrupted during the vacation season, from mid-July to mid-September (especially August) and from December 23 to January 6. Businessmen are advised to avoid Italy during these periods.

There are local public vacations on the Feast Day of the Patron Saint in each town. In Milan this falls on December 7 (St. Ambrose).

Hours of Business

Government offices are generally open from 08:30 to 13:45 Monday to Saturday. Senior staff sometimes return to their offices from 17:30 until 20:00 in the evening Monday to Friday and will see visitors by appointment.

Business houses in northern Italy are open usually from 08:30 to 12:45 and from 15:00 to 18:30, Monday to Friday; and from 08:30 to 12:45 on Saturday.

Business houses in central and southern Italy are usually open from 08:30 to 12:45 and 16:30 or 17:00 to 20:00, Monday to Friday; and from 08:30 to 12:45 on Saturday.

Banking hours are from 08:30 to 13:30, Monday to Friday. Post offices are open from 08:30 to 14:00, Monday through Saturday. Central post offices stay open until 21:00.

Shops have summer and winter hours. In summer (June through

September) they are open from 09:00 to 13:00 and from 16:30 to
20:00, Monday through Saturday. In winter (October through May)
they are open from 09:00 to 13:00 and reopen at 15:30 to 19:30,
Monday to Saturday.

Currency and Banking

The unit of currency in Italy is the lira (Lit.).

The state owns or controls 80% of the banks in Italy.

The all-powerful Bank of Italy (Banca d'Italia) is owned by the
banking sector which has no control over it.

Italian banking laws are very detailed and Italian bankers are quite
clever in figuring ways around the law. Yet Italian banking does not
include many of the normal U.S. services. Money market and clearing
house systems are minimal.

Banking is in the hands of a few powerful banks and no less than 24
Italian banks are among the world's 300 largest banks.

Italian banks are particularly good at international transactions (they
are the oldest banks in the world).

Foreign banks have had difficulty in establishing themselves in Italy
but four major U.S. banks are there.

Exchange Control
General

Foreigners may open external bank accounts, freely transferable to
any currency; capital accounts to finance Italian investments; and
investment accounts. The latter are best for investments in Italy
because once the investment has been approved funds may be freely
moved in and out of Italy.

Italy has a two-tier "commercial lira" and "financial lira" market.
The first is for commercial and "invisible" transactions (insurance,
tourism). The "financial lira" relates to capital movements (private
investment, financial credit, commercial credit).

Foreign investments in Italy are classified as "productive" or
"non-productive", with separate rules for each category.

"Productive" investments are those which produce (or expand the
production of) goods and services and which require investment in
capital equipment for an extended period. These enterprises may either
be wholly financed from foreign sources or have a mixture of Italian and
foreign capital.

"Non-productive" investments are portfolio investments and any
others not classified as "productive".

Italian companies and individuals may not accept loans from
foreigners without the prior approval of the Treasury.

The minimum period within which loan repayments must be made 181 and the maximum allowable rate of interest vary frequently. The Treasury usually allows liberal terms for long-term loans from foreign companies to their subsidiaries and for short-term loans within the EEC.

Capital

There are no restrictions on foreign capital transfers. One of the major benefits for foreign investors is that capital, interest and dividends may, with one exception, be freely repatriated (Italians are severely restricted from taking money out of Italy).

The exception is imported machinery. Here the transfer abroad of capital from investments in machinery may be made only from the proceeds of any subsequent disinvestment and not less than two years from the date of the investment.

Repatriation of "non-productive" funds (capital, interest and dividends) is restricted to an annual maximum of 8% of the capital invested. No remittances may be made within two years of the original investment and total remittances must not exceed the total foreign capital originally invested.

There are repatriation restrictions for imports and exports, license fees and royalties and foreign nationals' funds but they are not onerous.

Imports

Imports must usually be paid for within 360 days of customs clearance. If the importer wants to make advance payments against imports, he can only do so within 90 days before customs clearance. On imports from EEC countries, the deadline may be extended for five years. Italian exporters should not give more than 360 days credit from the date of customs clearance (although there are exceptions for EEC countries).

Foreign employees

There are no restrictions on the transfer of earnings abroad by foreign employees in Italy.

Transfers of currency from Italy can be made only after all taxes, personal and company, have been settled, unless guarantees are given to the revenue authorities.

Forms of Doing Business

A foreign investor may operate in Italy either through a branch of a foreign company, a sole proprietorship or an Italian company.

The various recognized business forms are governed by the Civil Code and are as follows:

1. Società per Azioni (S.p.A.)—corporations.
2. Società a Responsabilità Limitata (S.R.L.)—small private companies.

3. Filiale—branch office.
4. Società in nome collectivo (S.N.C.)—a partnership in which all partners are jointly and individually liable for partnership debts.
5. Società in accomandita per azioni (S.a.p.a.)—a partnership in which interests are represented by par value shares. It may contain general partners as in a S.N.C. and limited partners with liability restricted to their share participation.
6. Società in accomandita semplice (S.a.S.)—a limited partnership in which there must be at least one general and one limited partner.
7. Imprenditore individuale—sole proprietorship.

S.p.A. Companies

This is the form usually adopted by foreign investors. A Certificate of Incorporation (Atto Constitutivo) containing the information required by the Civil Code must be filed in the local court where the head office of the new company is located.

By-laws stating the company's objects and outlining its financial structure must also be filed. The company becomes operative after the court has approved the certificate, its deed has been filed in the Companies Register and the registration tax has been paid.

The Certificate of Incorporation must be published in the Foglio Annunci Legali (Legal News Bulletin) and the Bulletin of Companies and Partnerships (BUSA). The company must also be registered with the local Chamber of Commerce and its formation entered in the schedario generale delle azioni e delle obbligazioni (general file of shares and bonds) kept in Rome.

An S.p.A. must have at least two shareholders (who do not need to be Italian nationals or residents) and a minimum capital of Lit. 1 million. This must be subscribed in full and at least 30% must be deposited with the Banca d'Italia where it is held in a non-interest bearing account until the company has been incorporated. No deposits are required for subsequent capital increases. Where the original capital, or increase of capital, exceeds Lit. 500 million a special authorization from the Treasury is required. Shares must be registered, although companies located in Sicily, Sardinia and the Trentino-Alto-Adige region may, under certain conditions, issue bearer shares. Usually debentures may not exceed the paid-up capital of the company.

There is a registration tax on formation of the company and on any increases in its capital. Other formation costs include a 2% mortgage registration tax on capital contributions in the form of buildings and land; notaries' fees (they vary depending on the capital involved) from Lit. 60,000 to Lit. 200,000; and registration expenses at the local court are Lit. 45,000. Other taxes and expenses are nominal.

In all new S.p.A.'s the directors and the auditors must verify the value

183

of assets contributed in exchange for shares; and an expert appointed by the court must submit a sworn valuation statement which is attached to the Certificate of Incorporation. Should the values be reduced by more than 20%, the stated capital of the S.p.A. must be reduced proportionately.

Shares and Shareholders

Shares must have an assigned or par value. Share certificates must contain information including their value, the company's total capital and other items. Unless otherwise stipulated in its by-laws, a company's shares are usually freely transferrable. Ordinary shares normally carry voting rights of not more than one vote per share. Preference shares may have restricted rights. Not more than 50% of the issued capital may be restricted.

There are four classes of shares: azioni ordinarie (ordinary shares); azioni privilegiate (preference shares); azioni di godinento (deferred shares, which do not normally carry voting rights); azioni a favore dei prestatori di Lavoro (employees' shares).

At the time of incorporation a company must have at least two shareholders. After formation it may have only one shareholder who must then assume personal unlimited liability for the company's debts. Limited companies may be shareholders in other companies. Companies may not normally purchase their own shares nor shares of related companies.

Company Management
1. Directors

There are no legal requirements as to the nationality, residence or number of directors. Composition of the board of directors is specified in the Certificate of Incorporation or is determined by shareholders at a general meeting. Individual appointments are for three years and re-elections are possible. Directors may be removed at a shareholders' meeting. A director does not have to be a shareholder but must give a personal guarantee equal to 2% of the company's capital (or some smaller sum as the company's rules may determine) to cover liabilities he may incur during his period of office. Board meetings need not be held in Italy. Powers may be delegated to one or more managing directors.

2. Board of Auditors (Collegio Sindacale)

Every corporation must have three to five statutory auditors (sindaci) with two alternates. The first sindaci are named in the company's statutes and thereafter are elected for three-year periods at fixed rates of compensation.

Sindaci may be shareholders but may not be related to directors or employees. Companies with a capital of Lit. 50 million or more must select one sindaci (in a three-man board) or two sindaci (in a five-man board) from the official Register of Auditors. The functions of the sindaci are to ensure that the company is operating within the law, to supervise the directors, to safeguard shareholders' interests, to examine cash and securities periodically and to examine the annual accounts.

3. The shareholders

An annual general meeting must be held, usually not later than four months after the end of the company's financial year. The annual general meeting normally adopts the audited accounts, elects or re-elects directors and sindaci and fixes their pay. A quorum consists of shareholders representing at least 50% of the shares with full voting rights. Resolutions may be passed by a simple majority.

Shareholders may appoint proxies but only in writing. Directors and employees, however, are barred from acting as proxies. Shareholders may not vote on resolutions in which they have a personal interest, but their shares may be counted for quorum requirements.

Legal Reserves

Each company must accumulate a reserve by allocating at least 5% of its annual net profits until the reserve reaches 20% of the issued capital. Should the reserve be decreased by losses, the annual allocation must be re-established. If losses reach one-third of the initial capital there must be a proportionate reduction in the company's stated capital. If losses reduce the capital below Lit. 1 million, further capital must be paid in or the company must be changed to an S.R.L. Premiums paid for shares issued above their par value may not be distributed until the legal reserve has reached the required level.

S.R.L. Companies

For these companies the minimum capital required is Lit. 50,000. The same general principles apply as for an S.p.A. Capital is not represented by negotiable shares but is divided into quotas. These quotas cannot be for less than Lit. 1,000 each. They are recorded in a register of members and may usually be transferred.

An S.R.L. must have one or more directors, who must generally be shareholders. It must have a board of auditors (sindaci) if its capital is Lit. 1 million or more. It may not issue debentures or other bonds. The name of the company must indicate that it is an S.R.L.

Branch Office (Filiale)

Foreign companies may do business in Italy by setting up branch offices. Branches must be registered within 30 days of their

185

establishment. Registration consists of filing with the local Registrar of Enterprises, the company's certificate of incorporation, balance sheet, and the names and signatures of those authorized to act on behalf of the parent company. These documents must be notarized by an Italian consul in the country of origin and by the Ministry of Foreign Affairs in Rome. The branch must then register with the Chamber of Commerce which will give it a registration number. Failure to comply with these formalities means that the branch manager(s) bear(s) unlimited personal liability for the company. After registration the parent foreign company is liable for all debts and obligations incurred by the branch.

There are some disadvantages in the use of a branch. The parent company may be involved in inquiries on branch affairs, and it may be difficult to make local officials understand the nature of the business of the foreign parent.

Partnerships

Foreign companies and individuals may be partners in any of the three forms of partnership. Partnerships are governed by the Civil Code, the rules being almost identical to those for an S.p.A. They must be entered in the Companies Register and the local Chamber of Commerce, where the trading name, address and business must be recorded. Partnerships can act as legal entities, but generally a legal entity may be a partner only in a limited partnership. As in other countries, limited partners may in general take no part in the management of the partnership nor may their names appear in the firm's name.

The Italian Tax System

Italian tax legislation does not discriminate between Italians and foreigners. Taxes are divided into two categories:

a. taxes assessed on the property or income of individuals—"direct taxes"; and

b. taxes levied on the value of goods, transactions, or payments—"indirect taxes".

Taxes
1. Registration Tax

A wide variety of transactions are subject to registration and payment of registration tax.

For the incorporation of companies, formation of partnerships or joint ventures and for capital increases the registration tax is 5% for real estate and connected matters. This rate is reduced to 2% for industrial plants or facilities, and to 1% in other cases.

In the case of corporate mergers, the above rates are halved.

Foreign companies which establish branch offices in Italy are subject to a registration tax on that portion of their assets which are allocated for their Italian activities.

2. The Municipal Tax on Value Increases (INVIM)

A tax is imposed on increases in value of property when property rights are transferred. The rates vary from 3% to 30%.

Real estate management companies pay this tax every 10 years.

3. Value-Added Tax (IVA) Imposta sul Valore Aggiunto

The normal VAT rate is 12%, reduced to 6% for certain mass-consumption goods and services (some foods, pharmaceuticals, printed matter, and other information services) and increased to 18% for luxury goods.

VAT is not applied on exported goods, ships and aircraft or to the prices of international services or items connected with international trade.

The tax is payable in monthly instalments. The taxpayer may deduct the tax paid to his suppliers from his tax liability.

4. Personal Income Tax

Income tax is paid by individuals and by partners in proportion to their share of their businesses. Non-residents pay in proportion to their Italian income.

There are a number of fixed deductions. The net aggregate income is calculated as far as possible on documentary evidence. The rates are progressive and applied on successive income brackets, ranging from 10% for the first 2 million lire ($3,440) to 72% for income exceeding 500 million lire ($860,000).

5. Company Tax

This tax is payable by companies which have their head offices or their main activities in Italy.

Taxable income includes income from land and buildings, from business activities, capital gains realized, distributed and reported in the balance sheet; profits and income from shares.

The tax rate is proportional and amounts to 25%. It is reduced to 7.5% in the case of holding companies, and to 6.25% in the case of government-controlled holding companies.

Taxable income is calculated from the balance sheet or from the statement of accounts (excluding income from land, agriculture and building, which is calculated on estimated schedules).

187

6. Withholding Tax

Dividends are subject to a 10% withholding tax in the case of residents.

For non-residents the withholding tax is 30%. The double tax treaty with the U.S. reduces this rate to 15%.

7. Local Income Tax (ILOR)

This tax affects individuals, regardless of residence, partnerships and companies, in Italy and abroad. It applies to income from capital, land and buildings, agriculture and business.

Rates range from 8.9% to 14.2%, with deductions for individuals. The revenue is divided among municipalities, provinces and regions, and chambers of commerce.

8. The "Substitute" Tax on Interest

This tax is applied at different rates:

a. 30% on interest, not eligible for reduced rates;
b. 20% on interest on bonds and similar securities, issued by holding companies and by government agencies;
c. 15% on interest on bank and postal deposits and checking accounts;
d. 10% on interest on bonds and similar securities issued by banks or financial institutions.

In the case of individuals and partnerships the tax is withheld at the source at a flat rate with mandatory tax credit. Interest, therefore, is free from national and municipal income taxes and is not to be reported in income tax returns.

In the case of companies, the withholding is on an "on-account" basis credited against the national and municipal income taxes. Interest income therefore, is part of their taxable income and must be reported.

Accounting

Italian accounting, like its taxes, is not to be taken seriously.

Published annual reports usually differ greatly from the accounts submitted to the tax collector. There may be another set of accounts for management (the closest to the truth).

Italians guard their privacy with charming intensity.

Taxation is the major consideration in the preparation of accounts. Accounts are made to look plausible and to give a favorable tax position. Hidden reserves, secret bank accounts, non-existent liabilities, omitted sales reports and the understatement of assets are common. Taxes are often a matter for negotiation.

Depreciation is available for cases where profit is shown.

Consolidated accounts are not required and are rarely given.

Assets must be listed at cost.

Inventory is calculated on the LIFO (last in—first out) basis. Contingent liabilities need not be shown.

The equivalent of a C.P.A. is a dottore comercialista while a book-keeper is a ragioniere e perito commerciale.

EEC law will bring changes to Italy's accounting procedures.

Business Incentives

Italy offers broad investment incentives.

Up to 70% of the cost of a new plant can be obtained from the government on good terms for up to 15 years.

In the south the "Cassa per il Mezzogiorno" program offers the maximum benefits plus tax holidays for up to 10 years.

These programs vary from region to region and are designed to stimulate investment in underdeveloped areas like Sicily and Sardinia.

Stock Exchange

The Italian stock market is small and weak. 40% of the listed companies are government controlled and 30% are under foreign control. The Italian investor distrusts shares.

Money is more apt to be raised by bonds issued by banks than by public share offers.

The Milan Bourse plans to make the stock market a significant factor in Italy's financial industry but there is a long way to go.

Labor

Italy has an unhappy record of strikes and poor labor-management relations. There are three main trade unions and negotiations are done by collective bargaining on an industry-wide basis.

The cost of Italian labor has risen rapidly. Social security benefits are as high as anywhere in the world. In addition to the usual benefits, Italian workers get housing, accident and health insurance protection.

It is difficult to get rid of excess labor in Italy. Termination pay is excessive—even if the worker quits or is fired for cause. Italian companies sometimes form joint ventures with foreign companies based on the Italian company providing "free" labor as its capital contribution to the new enterprise in order to utilize surplus labor.

Payroll taxes are excessive and the cost of labor is almost double the apparent wages being paid. The employer must pay up to 50% of the employee's wage (the employee contributes 7%) and then give two to four months wages in annual bonuses.

Work permits for foreigners can be applied for at Italian consulates; or, if the applicant is in Italy, through the local police or Foreigners Office (Ufficio Straniere) with a letter from the prospective employer.

189

Permits are issued by the Ministry of Internal Affairs after approval of the Ministry of Labor and Social Welfare. Foreign workers have the same social security benefits as Italians.

Patents, Trademarks and Copyrights

Italian patents are good for 15 years and call for an annual fee increasing from Lit. 2000 to Lit. 35,000. The initial registration fee is based on the number of pages in the application.

Trademarks, like patents, are registered in the Central Patent Office and are valid for 20 years.

Copyrights are valid for 50 years after the author's death.

XII HOLLAND

Netherlands

KONINKRIJK DER NEDERLANDEN

1 red
2 white
3 blue

Total population 13,400,000

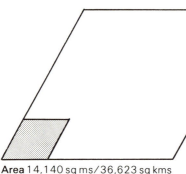

Area 14,140 sq ms / 36,623 sq kms

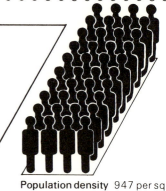

Population density 947 per sq m / 368 per sq km

Form of government Constitutional monarchy. Executive power is vested in the Monarch and a Cabinet headed by the Prime Minister. Legislative authority is exercised by the Monarch, Cabinet, and States General (Parliament). The States General has a First Chamber of 75 members, elected for 6 years by the Provincial Councils, and a Second Chamber, elected by direct, universal, and proportional suffrage. A Council of State functions as supreme advisory body to the Crown.

Head of state The Monarch / hereditary succession

Voting age 18 years

Public health Contributory state insurance scheme
13,558 doctors (1972)
69,500 hospital beds (1971)

Major imports Fuels and lubricants, foodstuffs, machinery, raw materials

Major exports Foodstuffs, chemicals, electrical goods, textiles, transport equipment

ivers
motorways
owns over 1 million
500,000-1 million
200,000-1 million

Amsterdam
The Hague
Rotterdam

0 |50 |100 |150 m
0 |100 |200 km

Mercantile marine 941
vessels/3,980,000 grt (1972)

Military personnel 121,200

Official language Dutch

School-leaving age 15 years

Higher education 13
institutes/130,000 places

Currency Guilder

Membership of international
organisations OECD, Council of
Europe, EEC, Benelux, the UN and
its agencies

Let's go Dutch

The Dutch have a saying, "God created the world but the Dutch made Holland".

A good part of Holland is the delta of the Rivers Rhine and Maas. By extensive construction of dikes to control ocean and river tides, the Dutch have extended and protected Holland. Without the dikes, half of the country would be under water at high tide. Together with its canals, the dikes give Holland a distinctive, romantic character.

Obviously Holland is flat and it has been known as the "Lowlands" (or Der Nederlands) throughout modern history. It has a total area of 13,500 square miles. With over 13 million people, Holland claims to be the most densely populated country in the world.

The national language is Dutch, but German, English and French are widely spoken. There are a number of English schools.

The largest cities are Amsterdam, Rotterdam and the Hague. Rotterdam is the world's largest port and serves as Europe's leading oil distribution and refining center. Twenty-five per-cent of Europe's oil flows through its six oil refineries. An additional giant oil terminal is under construction.

The Hague is the site of the World Court and the center of the Dutch Government.

Amsterdam is one of Europe's more interesting cities and is a major banking and commercial center.

While the Dutch are traditionally seafarers and farmers, today manufacturing is the mainstay of the economy. It accounts for over 40% of national income and the bulk of export products. Almost all of Holland's raw materials are imported. Holland has almost one-half of the total known natural gas reserves in Western Europe. Eighty-five per-cent of Dutch households are supplied with natural gas and the EEC relies to a great extent on Holland for it.

The Dutch are fine businessmen. Some of the world's largest companies are of Dutch origin. They include: Royal Dutch-Shell (petroleum and chemicals); Unilever (foodstuffs, detergents, toilet articles) and Philips (radio, television, electronics).

Holland's communications and transportation facilities are excellent. Amsterdam's Schipol airport is reputed to have the best duty free shop in the world.

Holland uses the metric system.

Foreigners driving in Holland should be aware of special lanes for the protection of cyclists and scooters. The large number of cyclists in the towns makes driving especially difficult at peak hours (approximately 08:00 to 09:00 and 16:30 to 18:00).

Taxis do not cruise for fares and must be called from a rank. There is usually one central number in each town from which they may be called.

Political Structure

The Netherlands (Holland) is a constitutional monarchy. It includes the Netherland Antilles in the Caribbean and Surinam in South America, which are autonomous states except in matters of foreign policy and defense. They all maintain a close political and economic relationship.

There are three main branches of the national government: the executive branch which represents the Crown; a two-chamber legislature and the judiciary. The Netherlands is divided into 11 provinces and 1,000 municipalities. The municipal and provincial governments are structural replicas of the national government. Holland is actually the name of two of its provinces (North and South Holland).

National government is the responsibility of the "Cabinet of Ministers". The Crown appoints a *Formateur* who consults with the political parties in order to propose to the Crown the names of the individuals to be appointed to ministerial positions. The *Formateur* is often selected as Prime Minister. The legislative body, called the "States General", consists of upper (Eerste Kamer) and lower (Tweede Kamer) chambers. The 150 members of the lower house are elected in general elections. The 75 upper house members are elected by the provincial governing bodies. There are some 14 political parties represented in Parliament.

Legislation is initiated in the lower chamber and has to be approved by the upper house and Crown to become law. There is also a constitutionally established "Council of State" which reviews legislation before it becomes binding.

Acts passed by both the upper and lower houses are the principal laws of the land. These include the Constitution which spells out the powers of government as well as the fundamental rights of citizens. These acts supersede laws enacted by provincial and municipal legislative bodies. Decrees are issued by the Crown with consent of the Cabinet and apply nationally. Treaties require approval of the two houses to be binding, and when they conflict with Acts, treaties are given precedence by the Courts.

195

Legal System

The courts are not empowered to nullify acts of other legislative bodies.

The Netherlands is a Civil Law country and judges are appointed for life.

There are 62 Cantonal Courts, 5 Courts of Appeal and a Supreme Court. The Cantonal Courts are the base of the legal pyramid and matters flow upwards from there.

The Supreme Court does not determine questions of fact. It deals exclusively with legal points. It also has authority to deal with offenses by government ministers, and matters on appeal from the Antilles and Surinam.

General Business Pointers

As a great trading nation, Holland welcomes foreign businessmen. Forty per-cent of foreign businesses in Holland come from the U.S. which is its third largest trading partner.

Hours of Business

The hours of business are as follows:

Government offices:	08:30 to 17:00 Monday to Friday
Banks:	09:00 to 15:00 Monday to Friday
Offices:	08:30 to 17:30 Monday to Friday
Factories:	07:30 or 08:00 to 16:30 or 17:00 Monday to Friday
Shops:	Usually 09:00 to 18:00

Vacations

The important vacations are:

New Year's Day
Easter Monday
HM Queen Juliana's Birthday (April 30)
Ascension Day
Whit Monday
Christmas Day
Boxing Day (December 26)

Generally, department and general trading stores close on Monday mornings and shops selling consumer goods on Wednesday afternoons. Some municipalities permit shops to stay open until 21:00 one day a week, or one day a month, usually on a Thursday or Friday.

Currency and Banking

The official unit of currency is the gulden (Fl), divided into 100 cents. It is also known as the guilder or florin.

The Dutch banking structure is simple and fairly free of onerous restrictions.

Holland has a full range of banking services and foreign banks can establish themselves without difficulty.

Six of the world's 300 largest banks are Dutch, they are:

Cooperative Centrale Raiffeissen—Boeren-Leenbank,

Algemene Bank Bederland,

Amsterdam—Rotterdam Bank,

Nederlandische Middenstandbank,

Mees & Hope Group, and Nederlandse Credietbank.

A number of U.S. banks have Dutch offices—mainly in Amsterdam.

Exchange Control

The government-owned Nederlandse Bank controls international financial transactions. A number of Dutch banks are licensed to administer international exchange payments. Specific permission for payments made "from time to time" is not required by the Nederlandse Bank, but information on these transactions must be provided to the government for balance of payments calculations. Special forms are provided for these reports.

International payments for most commercial transactions can be made through general license agents and banks. Incoming payments must be made in internationally convertible currency. Outgoing payments can be made in any currency.

Bank accounts can be opened without formality. It is customary for payments to be made in cash or by bank transfer (the giro system) rather than by personal checks. Bank charges are levied depending on the size and turnover of the account. Interest is paid on demand and time deposits.

Convertible guilder accounts may be maintained in Dutch banks by non-residents. They are useful for paying local bills while keeping funds in an easily transferable form. Temporary residents (residents for a period of up to three years) must obtain a license to transfer their Dutch earnings abroad. Permanent residents (residents over three years) need a different form of permission for each transfer. Both are generally freely given by the Nederlandse Bank.

Investments

A non-resident who wants to invest in land, buildings or business or make loans to a Dutch company must apply to the Nederlandse Bank for an "investment permit". These permits are easily obtained. Special permission from the Ministry of Economic Affairs is required for investments in manufacturing, engineering or the contracting businesses. The Ministry will want to know the type of business involved, its estimated annual world sales, number of employees, and the amount and origin of required capital.

No permit is needed to invest in manufacturing if the enterprise can be financed in Holland. In other cases the Nederlandse Bank decides what proportion of capital must be brought from abroad to finance a foreign-owned enterprise.

Once permission is obtained, payments by a Dutch subsidiary to its foreign parent of profits, license fees, royalties, loan interest, and proceeds from sale or liquidation of a Dutch enterprise can be made freely.

The Nederlandse Bank has special rules for investments by non-residents in certain non-manufacturing enterprises. A non-resident investor must bring into Holland a proportion of the enterprise's capital requirement for a period of more than one year. The sum must equal one-half of the investors interest in the enterprise. It can be in the form of money or property.

Non-residents and foreign corporations need Central Bank approval to set up or acquire a financial subsidiary. Approval may depend on the minimum authorized capital being about $350,000 and an undertaking that no capital or loans will be acquired from Dutch corporations or residents.

Repatriation of Funds

Capital from loans or the sale of shares can be repatriated by non-residents without restriction, if an exchange permit was issued for the original investment.

Loans between residents and non-residents do not require approval if they are for Fl. 100,000 or less.

Foreign Employees

There is no restriction on the repatriation of earnings of foreign nationals employed in Holland.

Forms of Doing Business

A non-resident can do business in Holland through any recognized business form. There are three basic alternatives: 1) a branch of foreign corporation; 2) a choice from four kinds of partnerships; or 3) a corporation.

1. Branches

A Dutch branch of a foreign enterprise is treated as part of the parent and not as a separate legal entity. This means that all the rights and obligations of the branch are attributed to the parent. The branch is subject to Dutch law on its operations in the Netherlands.

2. Partnerships

There are four kinds of Dutch partnerships.

a. The General partnership (*Vennootschap Onder Firma*) is similar to a U.S. partnership and has a minimum of two partners using a common name for the business. It must be organized for business purposes rather than professional services. The partners are both jointly and independently liable for claims against the partnership.

b. The limited partnership (*Commonditaire Vennootschap*) has one or more general partners with unlimited liability and at least one partner with limited liability. A limited partner's liability extends only to the amount of his capital contribution. The general partners must manage the firm. If a limited partner takes an active part in management he may lose his limitation of liability benefit.

c. There is also a partnership with shares (*Commanditaire Vennootschap op Aandelen*). This is a limited liability partnership in which the capital is divided into transferable shares similar to a corporation.

d. The civil partnership (*Maaschap*) is used by professional firms. The partners are individually liable to creditors.

3. Corporations

There are two types of Dutch corporations.

The first is the *Naamloze Vennootschap*, or public company, abbreviated N.V. It is similar to an American company.

The second type is a closely held corporation, *Besloten Vennootschap*, abbreviated B.V. It was created in 1968 to bring Dutch company law more in line with other EEC countries.

All companies are required to use either the N.V. or the B.V. corporate designation in their name.

Letterheads must show the company's registration number and indicate the commercial register in which the company has been listed.

Companies
Formation

The formation of both N.V.'s and B.V.'s requires two incorporators who subscribe to a minimum of 20% of the authorized share capital of the company and pay for at least 10% of the capital at the time of incorporation. There is no minimum authorized capital required for incorporation although shares must reflect at least a nominal par value. Shares may be purchased with non-cash assets but "services rendered" is not acceptable as payment. The purchase of shares with non-cash assets prior to incorporation must be stated in the articles of the company or the buyer may get a demand for a second payment. Purchases made after incorporation need only be reported in the company's annual financial statement. Incorporators and shareholders

199

may be of any nationality.

Before incorporation a certificate of "no objection" must be issued by the Ministry of Justice. Usually a Dutch notary is retained to apply to the Ministry for the certificate. (The Dutch notary also customarily prepares and processes articles of incorporation, by-laws, partnership agreements, as well as administering estates and conveyancing of real property.) The registered office of the corporation must be in the Netherlands though this need not be its principal place of business.

Shares and Shareholders

An N.V. corporation may issue either bearer shares which are negotiable or registered shares which are non-negotiable. Preferred and cumulative preferred shares can also be issued. All shares in Dutch corporations have voting rights although voting agreements (that separate voting and financial rights) are allowed. Dutch law also recognizes "priority shares" which are vested with special privileges such as the right to veto amendments to the company's articles or to participate in decisions to change the capital of the company.

Unlike the N.V. corporation, the B.V. does not issue share certificates but maintains a register which records the names and addresses of shareholders and the amount of their holdings. B.V. shares may only be transferred in accordance with the company's by-laws.

Accounts

An N.V. is required to file an annual profit and loss statement and balance sheet with the trade register of the corporation's registered office.

The B.V. is generally not required to publish its annual financial accounts or to use a certified accountant to prepare or audit its reports.

The B.V. must publish a summary balance sheet (this does not include a profit and loss statement) only if its assets amount to no less than Fls. 8 million and it has, together with its subsidiaries, 100 employees or more.

Fees Payable

The fees when the Articles of Association (*statuten*) are filed is $2\frac{1}{4}\%$ of the paid and subscribed shares, plus $\frac{1}{4}\%$ on the remaining issued shares. There is a further fee of $2\frac{1}{4}\%$ on remaining issued shares when they are paid for. Legal fees for forming a company are usually based on the initial authorized share and loan capital. The minimum total of all fees payable on formation of a company with initial capital of Fls. 1 million would be about $6,900.

Company Management

Dutch law attempts to establish a two-tier structure of management. Managers or managing directors (*directie*) are responsible for day-to-day business operations. The company's articles may also stipulate that one or more supervisory officers (*commissarissen*) be appointed to advise and supervise the directors.

Rules Applying to Large Business Corporations

There is a distinction in Dutch law between large and small business corporations—irrespective of whether they are N.V. or B.V. Certain restrictions are placed on large corporations. A large corporation is one whose subscribed capital and reserves are at least Fl. 10 million (about $3.5 million) and which has at least 100 employees and a workers' council. There are exceptions for certain holding companies if the majority of employees work outside of Holland. The law is designed to give the workers more management control. This is achieved by appointing a number of the supervisory directors to represent the workers.

Taxes
Company Taxes

There are a number of features in the Dutch tax laws which make Dutch-based finance companies attractive.

There is no Dutch withholding tax on interest paid by these companies on bonds, notes and other debt obligations. Also, because of double tax treaties, interest paid by foreigners to a Dutch-based financing subsidiary is often free of withholding tax or subject to reduced rates of tax in the debtor's country. These subsidiaries can take out Euro-currency loans and relend these funds to finance business operations of the parent or other related companies without incurring heavy tax obligations. Another attraction is that there are no Dutch inheritance or estate taxes levied on debt obligations of non-residents. This is particularly interesting to U.S. businessmen because of the favorable tax treaty terms between the U.S. and Holland.

The standard rate of withholding tax is 30%—reduced by treaty to 15%. Foreign source dividends received by a Netherlands company are subject to only a 5% withholding tax in the U.S. if the Dutch company owns at least 25% of the U.S. company.

Double taxation agreements are in force between the Netherlands and most western nations. Dividends paid by Dutch corporations are subject to 25% withholding tax unless a lower rate is granted by treaty. A recipient company resident in the U.S., Canada or the U.K. is subject to a withholding rate of 15%.

A finance subsidiary is presumed to have received taxable income for   201 its business efforts. The Dutch tax authorities have devised a liberal system for calculating taxable income. Interest paid by Dutch corporations is tax deductible. The subsidiary may subtract the interest paid for its borrowings from the interest it receives from relending these funds. However, the overall net taxable income in any tax year must not be less than a given percentage of its total equity and any borrowed funds. This "spread" can be as low as 1/8 of 1%.

The Central Bank also determines the maximum debt to equity ratio allowed. The normal ratio is 10:1. Ratios of 50:1 and 100:1 have been permitted. However, consideration must also be given to prevailing policies in the parent company's country. In the U.S. the Treasury will not recognize a financial subsidiary of a U.S. corporation if its debt-equity ratio is more than 5:1. As recognition brings certain tax advantages, U.S. companies must bear the 5:1 ratio figure in mind when doing business abroad.

Dutch corporation tax is levied on companies, partnerships with shares, and mutual insurance companies. The rate is 49% (inclusive of a 3% surcharge) of net profits (except for a reduced rate granted to companies whose net profits are under Fls. 50,000). A non-resident corporation is generally not liable to tax except on income from a fixed place of business in the Netherlands (such as a branch office), income from property or interest on mortgages in the Netherlands. Royalty payments received by foreign companies or payments received under profit-sharing rights from Dutch enterprises are not taxable.

Company tax applies equally to all net profits, including capital gains. Profits earned abroad are exempt if they are subject to tax in a foreign country. Expense deductions include interest payments, allowable business expenses (employee compensation, director's attendance fees, travel expenses, interest, royalties, import duties, rent, foreign taxes paid, etc.), depreciation charges, additions to reserves, and profit-sharing bonuses.

Tax losses can be carried back one year or forward six years. Losses sustained in the first six years of operations can be carried forward indefinitely. Recent legislation restricts purchases of tax loss companies. It prohibits the use of any loss carryover connected with discontinued operations of the acquired company.

Dividends, received by Dutch "portfolio" holding companies and by other resident companies which own 5% or more of the shares in the dividend paying company, are exempt from corporate tax if the shares were held from the start of any given fiscal year. Other exceptions allow the shareholder to qualify for the exemption if the shares are held for reasons integral to the business operations of the holding company or if they were acquired with the public interest in mind.

Special rules apply to mutual funds where the exemption regulations relate to the fund's loans, distribution of profits, amount of non-resident holdings in the funds and holdings by resident shareholders through foreign intermediaries.

Dividends from foreign companies are tax free if the foreign company is taxed in a similar manner to Dutch companies and if the recipient corporation's ownership of the foreign shares is not in the nature of a portfolio investment. Where the activities of the two companies are similar the portfolio investment question does not arise.

Both tangible and intangible assets may be depreciated. The "straight line" method is usually used but the "declining balance" system is permitted for assets with greater wear in early life. Annual depreciation is based on the lesser of either the physical life or the economic life of the asset.

Capital assets may be given special treatment where they are sold with the intention of replacing them. The proceeds from such sales can be placed in reserve accounts for four years and the amount of the reserves set off against the cost price of the new capital assets.

One feature of the Dutch accounting practices is the system of valuing fixed assets according to their replacement value rather than by the traditional cost basis method of valuation.

Personal Income Tax

Dutch residents are subject to tax on all their income. Residents who receive income from abroad are exempted if they are taxed in the source country. A number of factors are used to determine Dutch residence. Most important are whether the taxpayer's family and main sources of income are in the Netherlands. Non-residents are taxed on Dutch income at the same rates as resident taxpayers.

Taxable income includes wages, fees, royalties, income from property, industrial or trading profits, dividends, income from securities and interest. Each income category is permitted certain deductions.

The rates of tax are laid down in schedules contained in the Personal Income Tax Act 1964. The tax rates are progressive and apply whether or not the taxpayer was subject to tax during the entire year. They are subject to a surcharge of 3%. There are four tax schedules that apply to the following individual taxpayers:

SCHEDULE 1   All taxpayers except those in the other schedules.
SCHEDULE 1A   Taxpayers not in the next two schedules, and who are over 40 at the end of the calendar year.
SCHEDULE II   Taxpayers not in SCHEDULE III who were married and lived together part of the year. Taxpayers over 65 at the end of the year. Married taxpayers not living together but who either have been married for at least five years during which

period they lived together or whose marriage has produced children.

SCHEDULE III Taxpayers who have one or more dependent children—subdivided according to the number of children. Tax relief is given for each child by way of reduced tax rates.

The following are selected examples of 1972 tax rates, inclusive of the surcharge:

Taxable Income (Fls.)	I	IA	II	III (2 Children)
100,000	56,377	53,148	49,918	48,516
65,000	31,638	26,267	26,896	25,613
32,250	10,886	9,740	8,594	7,631
22,000	5,861	5,107	4,353	3,590
14,300	2,883	2,430	1,976	1,397

A married woman's income is added to her husband's but she receives a special deduction of:

1. The first Fls. 1,046 of earned income, plus
2. 20% of earned income over Fls. 1,046 up to a total deduction of Fls. 4,184.

There are liberal child allowances. These are available to non-residents only if their country grants a similar allowance to Dutch residents.

Certain kinds of personal income are taxed at lower rates. These include profits gained through transferring, closing or liquidating a business and profits from the sale of shares or certificates of a corporation in which the taxpayer had a "substantial interest".
A "substantial interest" is not less than one-third of a corporation held either directly or indirectly through a family group within five years of the sale. In addition the taxpayer personally (or with his wife) must have held at least 7% of the corporation's outstanding stock during this period. The tax rate applied to this income is 20%.

There is a Dutch "net wealth" tax levied annually at a rate of 0.8% on the market value of an individual's assets. Exempted from gross wealth calculation are household goods, furniture, art objects, annuity policies that are not business assets and insurance policies whose yearly premiums are paid. The net wealth of a married woman is added to that of her husband. Non-residents are subject to wealth tax only on the value of certain assets located in the Netherlands. These include assets of a permanent foreign business establishment in Holland but exclude the net wealth reflected by the company's shares. Immovable property and mortgage loans are also included for net wealth computations. Deductions can be taken for expenses directly related to these assets.

The standard deduction permitted is Fls. 40,000 for a single taxpayer and Fls. 55,000 for a married couple. There are additional deductions for persons over 65 and for dependent children.

VAT

The Netherlands also imposes a value-added tax (called Belasting Torgevoigde waarde, or BTW) on the manufacture, distribution, and sale of most goods produced in Holland. Imports and exports are also taxed but the export tax is refundable. The standard rate of VAT is 14%. Some basic commodities are granted a 4% rate.

Transfers of real estate are subject to a 5% transfer tax.

Insurance premiums and stock transfers are also subject to tax at 4% and 12% respectively.

The tax year is the calendar year. Returns are due April 1 or within six months of the end of the company's fiscal year and you are taxed provisionally at 80% of the previous year's tax.

Investment Incentives

Government subsidies are granted for investment in certain industries and factories. Grants are provided both for acquisition of industrial sites and toward the cost of construction.

Investment grants are usually for 25% of the investment up to Fl. 3,000,000. In certain cases the government may take a stake in the venture. Long-term (15 years) low interest loans are also available.

Under the Dutch freeport system no import duty, excise or turnover tax is charged on goods brought into Holland for re-exportation after processing. Freeport facilities for warehousing and storage of these goods are available throughout the country.

Labor

Work permits are renewable annually and should be obtained from regional labor offices. Skilled workers or managers are usually granted permits without difficulty.

The usual working week is 40 hours in offices and 45 in factories. There is a minimum wage for workers over 24.

Dutch labor relations are excellent. Unions are based first on an industry wide system and then by religion.

Extensive and expensive social security benefits are the rule. All workers get at least two weeks paid vacation and bonuses.

Citizens of EEC countries, Americans and many other nationalities do not need a visa to enter Holland. If a visitor wants to stay longer than three months then he must apply to the local police for a residence permit within eight days of his arrival. Once this permit is granted, the holder becomes a resident for tax and social security purposes.

Stock Market

The Amsterdam stock market is not large by U.S. standards.
A number of large foreign companies are listed on the exchange. To be
listed a company must have a paid up capital of Fl. 500,000 and its
shares must be widely held. Full disclosure rules apply to public issues
of shares.

Real Estate

The Netherlands is a crowded country and foreign investment in real
estate is not encouraged. The government has programs to discourage
developments in Amsterdam and to encourage them outside the
populated areas.

Patents, Trademarks and Copyrights

Patents are valid for 20 years and are not issued until an exhaustive
examination of the application and Patent Office records has been made.
Patents can be extended for another 20 years. Patent fees are payable
annually and are progressive from Fl. 225 to Fl. 1,250.

Trademarks are governed by the Benelux Uniform Law on
Trademarks which governs Belgium and Luxembourg as well.
Trademarks must be registered in the Benelux Register and are valid for
10 years and renewable. Registration does not create title to a trademark.

Copyrights are valid for a period of 50 years after the author's death.

Introduction

The Netherlands Antilles, together with Surinam and the Netherlands itself constitute the Kingdom of the Netherlands. Each partner of the Kingdom is autonomous but matters of international interest are directed from Holland. Close economic, political and commercial links are maintained between the three areas.

The civil and commercial laws of all three are co-ordinated under an Agreement of Concordance.

The Netherlands Antilles are two groups of islands. One group consists of Saba, St. Eustatius and a portion of St. Maarten (the other part is French) and is located 10 miles east of Puerto Rico. The second group, about 600 miles to the southwest and lying off the coast of Venezuela, is made up of Aruba, Bonaire and Curacao. The total population of all the islands is approximately 225,000.

The capital is Willemstad, in Curacao, the largest island of the group. It is here that many of the major banks, trust companies and law firms are based. The Netherlands Antilles is an associate member of the EEC.

The islands are popular as tropical resorts. Most residents are multilingual. The languages most commonly spoken are the local Papiamentu and Dutch, English and Spanish.

Air and shipping connections are excellent as are mail, telephone, telegraph and telex services.

The Netherlands Antilles (particularly Curacao and Aruba) are important shipping and airline junctions for traffic between Europe, North America, and South America. Aruba and Curacao have created "free zones" for storing and transfer of goods. Shell Oil and Standard Oil of New Jersey maintain large oil refineries in Curacao, Willemstad is a major bunkering port.

Favorable tax laws attract investment companies, financial subsidiaries, patent and copyright holding companies and real estate companies.

The U.S., U.K. and Denmark have double tax treaty arrangements with the Netherlands Antilles. Internal laws within the Dutch Kingdom regulate taxation between the three Dutch partners. These double tax "combination" features make the Netherlands Antilles a very desirable "tax haven", particularly for U.S. business, which can take advantage of both the Netherlands and the Netherlands Antilles laws in one business program.

Currency

The basic unit of currency is the Netherlands Antilles florin, abbreviated "N.A.Fls.".

207

Exchange Control

International financial transactions are subject to approval of the Foreign Exchange Control Board. Companies formed by non-residents with foreign capital which are not actively engaged in local trade or business can obtain a general license to freely transfer their capital and profits from overseas operations.

The Dutch Antilles also offer a "free zone" in which licensed corporations may import and export goods, duty free, or store, pack, assemble and process those goods free of duty.

Companies

A corporation is called "naamloze vennootschap", abbreviated N.V. It requires at least two founder shareholders who need not be either resident or domiciled in the Antilles. The founders must subscribe for at least 20% of the authorized capital of the N.V. Shares must have a par value and may be either bearer or registered shares.

Before commencing operations, the corporation must apply to the local office of the Director of Social and Economic Affairs for a business license and a director's license for each managing director. A non-resident who intends to become a resident must secure a permit from the immigration office. A further license, for relief from exchange control regulations (for companies operating abroad) should be obtained from the foreign exchange department of the Bank von de Nederlandse Antilles. All these licenses are readily available.

Company Tax and Finance

Tax rates range from 27% to 34%. However, there are special rates for investment, patent and copyright companies of 2.4%–3.0% of profits; with a total exemption for capital gains.

Investment Companies

An investment company is one whose central activity is to invest in securities, bonds and interest bearing debt obligations. Copyright and patent companies normally derive income from the sale or licensing of rights in copyrights, patents, designs, secret processes, trademarks, film royalties and rentals and use of industrial or scientific equipment. They may also exploit interests in natural resources and property.

While the subject is quite complex, there can be great tax advantages for U.S. companies in using Netherlands and Netherlands Antilles subsidiaries, as the double tax treaties with these areas are the most liberal known in the U.S. Dividends, interest and royalties from the U.S. are subject to a 30% U.S. withholding tax, in addition to the 2.4% to 3.0% Netherlands Antilles tax. This withholding rate may be reduced to 15% if the remaining shares of the recipient Netherlands Antilles corporation are: a) wholly owned by individual residents of the Netherlands Antilles, or b) wholly owned by Netherlands corporations or individuals resident in the Netherlands.

There is also a tax option feature whereby the recipient Dutch Antilles company can accept the Netherlands Antilles profit tax at a higher rate (15% for dividends and 24% to 30% for interest and royalties) and receive a reduced U.S. withholding rate of 15%.

Other tax incentives applicable to investment companies:

1. Capital gains are tax exempt. However, capital losses are not deductible for corporate tax purposes.
2. Distribution of profits in the form of stock of another company, received by a Netherlands Antilles investment company, is tax free if it is stock of the other company itself, and the company is listed on a stock exchange or is publicly traded.
3. Five-year loss 'carry overs" are allowed.

A Netherlands Antilles company can also be utilized as a holding company by its foreign-based parent, and can elect to be taxed as an investment company.

Other types of companies are subject to the same corporate tax rates on their dividend income from U.S. sources.

Financial subsidiaries based in the Netherlands Antilles are taxed in an almost identical manner to investment companies. One difference is that the financial subsidiary may deduct from its taxable income interest due and paid on its loans to banks, and also interest on bonds, notes and debentures.

Patents and Copyrights

Patent-holding and copyright companies based in the Netherlands Antilles are taxed at 2.4% to 3.0% on net income, and are free from capital gains tax. Like the investment companies the source and kind of income they receive, as well as the ownership of their stock, may affect their tax position.

Netherlands Antilles corporations are also granted special tax rates for income derived from property located outside the Netherlands Antilles and capital gains from its sale.

There is no withholding tax on dividends and interest paid by a Netherlands Antilles corporation to its non-resident stockholders.

The general picture for withholding tax on the royalty income of these companies from U.S. sources is either nil or 30% depending upon the nature of the income.

The tax on "duty free zone" companies is one-third of the standard 27% to 34% rate, plus a 15% surtax on the profits tax figures.

There are also liberal tax incentives to attract new industry and hotels, for the development of fallow land in the islands and for shipping and

209

airline companies.

Personal Taxation

Non-resident individuals who are not engaged in a trade or business in the Netherlands Antilles are not taxable there. The exception is the individual who at anytime within five years has owned directly or through his family, 25% of the issued shares of a Netherlands Antilles corporation. However, even these individuals will be free from tax if their ownership is in an investment or patent-holding company.

No estate tax is levied on a non-resident stock-holder of a Netherlands Antilles corporation.

XIII LUXEMBOURG

Luxembourg

GRAND-DUCHÉ DE LUXEMBOURG

1
2
3

1 red
2 white
3 blue

Total population 345,000

Area 999 sq ms/2,586 sq kms

Population density 345 per sq m/133 per sq km

Form of government Constitutional monarchy. Executive power is exercised by the Grand-Duke and the Cabinet under a Prime Minister. Legislative power is vested in the 56-member Chamber of Deputies. Deputies are elected for 5 years by direct, proportional, and universal suffrage. A 21-member Council of State, with members chosen for life, functions alongside the Chamber of Deputies and the Cabinet. It can be dissolved by the the Grand-Duke.

Head of state The Monarch/hereditary succession

Voting age 18 years

Public health Compulsory contributory state insurance scheme 362 doctors (1970) 4,289 hospital beds (1970)

Major imports Mineral products, machinery, electrical equipment, textile products, metals

Major exports Textile products, clothing, steel, tyres, engines, chemical products

Luxembourg

0 |50 |100 |150 m
0 |100 |200 km

Military personnel 550

Official language French

School-leaving age 15 years

Currency Luxembourg Franc

Membership of international organisations Benelux, OECD, EEC, Council of Europe, the UN and ts agencies

It's smaller than Rhode Island

Luxembourg is one of the world's smallest countries. Yet it is famous as a major international banking and investment center and is a fully fledged member of the EEC. It is situated in the heart of the Common Market, at the point where the French, German and Belgian borders meet. Its proper title is The Grand Duchy of Luxembourg (there really is a Grand Duke). Its land area is only 999 square miles but it is part of a large economic region extending into Lorraine (France) and the Saar basin (Germany).

The population is 350,000. About 48% of the people are employed in industry and 9% in agriculture. The rest work in commercial and service businesses. The country enjoys one of the highest standards of living in Europe. The vast majority of the people are Roman Catholic.

The capital is Luxembourg City, with a population of 80,000. The other "large" city is the mining and steel-making center of Esch-sur-Alzette, with a population of 29,000.

The northern region of Luxembourg is mountainous, while the south is flatter and rich in iron ore deposits. Iron, steel, chemicals, agriculture and tourism, in addition to international financial and banking services, are its main income-producing activities.

Almost one-fifth of its residents are foreign, due to the large number of Luxembourg-based international holding companies, and the use of Luxembourg City as the site for several EEC headquarters. These include the European Court of Justice and the European Investment Bank. The European Monetary Cooperation Fund will also be based in Luxembourg.

Over 80 banks and 120 mutual funds have offices in Luxembourg.

Besides its EEC membership, the Grand Duchy is also a part of the European Iron and Steel Community, the Benelux group of countries (economic treaty between Belgium, the Netherlands and Luxembourg) and the Union Economique Belgo-Luxembourgeoise.

There are major rail, highway and air links between Luxembourg and the rest of Europe. Icelandic Airlines uses Luxembourg as its European terminal for flights to the U.S. on a non-standard fare basis.

The official legislative, administrative and judicial language is French but the commercial language and the language of most of the newspapers is German. The people of Luxembourg speak Letzeburgesch, a language of mixed German-French origin, amongst themselves.

A knowledge of French and English is usually sufficient for the visiting businessman.

The services of a translator may be obtained, for a fee, from the Luxembourg Chamber of Commerce.

Luxembourg uses the metric system.

Government

The Grand Duke exercises executive power through a ministerial council (Council of State), which in turn is responsible to the Chamber of Deputies.

There are seven ministers and two secretaries of state.

Legislative power is shared by the Grand Duke and the Chamber of Deputies. Both the Chamber of Deputies and the Grand Duke must agree before new laws can be enacted. Laws have to be submitted for "advice" to the 21 members of the Council of State and to the pertinent professional and social bodies of which there are 56.

One deputy is elected for every 5,500 persons for a five-year term.

Legal System

The judiciary is independent. Judicial power belongs exclusively to the Courts and Tribunals (with the exception of the Grand Ducal "right of mercy").

The country is divided into two judicial districts and 12 cantons. Both judicial districts have one Tribunal responsible for civil, commercial and criminal affairs. Each of the 12 cantons has a Justice of the Peace presiding over minor civil, commercial and criminal offences. The High Court of Justice in Luxembourg is the highest Court of Appeal. Crimes are adjudicated by the "Cour d'Assises" composed of three members of the High Court of Justice and three members of the district tribunal. There is no provision for jury trials in Luxembourg.

Business Hours

Hours of business:

Commercial establishments: 08:00 to 12:00 and
14:00 to 18:00
Monday to Friday.

Government offices: 09:00 to 12:00 and
14:00 to 17:00
Monday to Friday.

Banks: 09:00 to 12:00 and
14:00 to 16:30
Monday to Friday.

215

Most businesses close on the afternoon of Shrove Tuesday, the Eve of All Saints' Day, Christmas Eve and New Year's Eve.

If a public vacation falls on a Sunday, the Monday following is generally observed instead.

Vacations

New Year's Day
*Shrove Monday
Easter Monday
Labor Day
Ascension Day
Whit Monday
Birthday of HRH the Grand Duke
Assumption Day
*Schobermess (Luxembourg Fair)
All Saints' Day
*All Souls' Day
Christmas Day
Boxing Day

Although the vacations marked with an asterisk * are not official, many businesses etc., close on these days.

Currency and Banking

The Luxembourg franc (L.Fr.) has the same value as the Belgian franc.

Ten per-cent of the national income is earned from taxes on banking operations. Luxembourg has experienced a tremendous upsurge in its banking and financial activity as European business has expanded. Because of its central location, its EEC membership and the tax advantages of its holding company legislation, foreign banks have been quick to take advantage of the opportunities offered by Luxembourg. U.S. banks are well represented.

The country is truly an international banking center without any political bias.

The authority for licensing banks rests with the Commissariat au Controle des Banques. New banks require a fully paid up capital of L.Fr. 100 million and must have at least one representative in Luxembourg. The Commission exercises careful control over banks under its jurisdiction.

The unique feature of the Luxembourg banking system is that almost 70% of deposits in the country are in foreign assets.

Exchange Control

Luxembourg has a two-tier foreign exchange market system identical to Belgium. There is the official market used mainly for foreign trade and the free market which acts as the financial market (investments).

Luxembourg has very liberal policies for free international transfer of funds. The Institut Belgo-Luxembourgois du Change (IBLC) controls all foreign exchange transactions for Belgium and Luxembourg. Investment in Luxembourg or Belgium can be made without approval. However, IBLC approval is needed if a foreign-owned company wants to acquire a company listed on the Belgium or Luxembourg stock exchange for a price exceeding B.Fr. 100 million.

Capital can be repatriated from Luxembourg without restriction at the free market exchange rate. An investor may also apply to the IBLC for a "transfer of capital and profit guarantee". If granted, the prevailing exchange rate at the time of repatriation will apply to such transfers.

There are no restrictions on the amount of foreign or local currency which may be taken into or out of Luxembourg.

Because of the unfamiliarity with Luxembourg money in other countries, it is advisable to change it before leaving the country.

Generally, export payments from Belgium and Luxembourg must be made within six months and import payments must be received within three months prior to shipment or three months after the import date.

The earnings of foreign nationals in Belgium and Luxembourg are freely transferable to other countries. Dividends can be paid to non-residents in their native currency. Foreigners can invest in securities and real estate in both countries.

Forms of Doing Business

Luxembourg financial and business operations are similar to those of Belgium (Chapter IV), except for their holding company features. Other businesses require a government permit before operations begin. Permits are obtained from the Ministry of Economic Affairs for a fee of L.Fr. 500. The Certificate of Incorporation of a company must be notarized and published in the official gazette. There is a 10% stamp tax on the transfer of shares. Notary fees and printing can be expensive.

All companies must register themselves at the Tribunal of Commerce and pay a registration tax.

By far the most important form of Luxembourg business entity is the S.A. (Societe Anonyme) holding company.

A minimum of seven founder shareholders are needed to form an S.A. company. These may be foreign individuals or companies. The articles are prepared by a notary and published in the "Memorial du Grand Duche de Luxembourg". Capital must be fully subscribed and at least 20% paid in prior to incorporation. There is no minimal capital requirement. Incorporation fees include a 1% capital registration tax on total contributed capital and a 0.36% subscription tax on the nominal

217

values of shares and bonds issued by the company. Registered or bearer shares are allowed and with minor exceptions they may be freely transferred. There is no par value requirement.

The registered office of the company must be in Luxembourg, and the annual shareholders meeting held there. Directors' meetings may be held elsewhere.

Luxembourg holding companies are famous for the tax and financing advantages they offer international investors. The main types of holding companies are the standard holding company, mixed holding company, financial holding company, investment management company, and finance company. Holding companies are almost always in the form of S.A. companies and must comply with the S.A. formation requirements.

A holding company is a company whose main purpose is to invest in other companies and to hold, administer and develop those interests.

Luxembourg holding companies are permitted to hold and deal in negotiable securities, to acquire, license and sell patents, and to lend funds to companies in which the holding company has an interest. A holding company may pay dividends and bond interest, free of withholding tax.

Standard holding companies are prohibited from being active members of partnerships (though they may be a "sleeping partner" in a partnership limited by shares), from carrying on any industrial or manufacturing activities, from operating public commercial businesses, from acting as banks, from owning real estate (although they may own shares in a real estate company) and they may not purchase the goodwill or know-how of any business.

A mixed holding company may carry on industrial or commercial activities but then it will not qualify for most of the special tax benefits received by holding companies.

A financial holding company is useful for the issue or sale of bonds or for floating loans in other countries since there is no withholding tax on the interest paid on them. This kind of company is often formed by a "group" of companies as a vehicle to raise funds for the group. It may make loans to the companies in the group if it meets these requirements: it must be an S.A. company; the group of companies must be named in its Articles as founders; it must issue registered shares which remain in the possession of the founder companies; it must own some shares or bonds issued by these companies or their subsidiaries; and, finally, its Articles must prohibit the use of its funds outside the group. Americans first took advantage of Luxembourg's facilities by creating financial holding companies there. Through these companies they financed the investment programs of their subsidiary companies in Europe. The first financial holding company to be incorporated in

Luxembourg was Mobil Oil Holdings. Industrial groups from many other countries followed the American lead.

Holding companies can borrow amounts up to 10 times the value of their capital and relend the entire issue without any reserves.

Financial holding companies were instrumental in creating the Eurobond market. From 1963, when New York was closed to issuers of foreign loans (due to the creation of Interest Equalization Tax to curb U.S. investments abroad), the Eurobond market replaced the American international financial market. First the European subsidiaries of American firms, then international companies from other countries, raised loans on the "Euromarket". Most loans were denominated in dollars (hence, "Eurodollars").

Another important use of Luxembourg holding companies is by *international investment funds* (mutual funds) which want to retain flexibility to invest internationally as well as collect and accumulate income, without incurring tax liability.

Where a syndicate of companies or private investors want to invest in several countries, a neutral, low-tax Luxembourg holding company is an ideal base for the joint venture.

Multinationals and promoters of large investment projects make great use of the holding company as a financing vehicle. An example is the Adela holding company (Adela Investment Company S.A.) incorporated in Luxembourg in 1964, in which big multinational groups such as Shell, Philips, Nestlé, Krupp, Hitachi and others, participated. The purpose of the Adela-Investment Company was to promote investments in Latin America and, by doing so, to sustain economic growth there.

Loans may also be made through a *"controlling interest" holding company* which is a company formed to manage subsidiaries in which it holds a dominant interest. A "controlling interest" also exists when management control is exercised over affiliates and the holding company owns at least 25% of those affiliates.

Loans to holding companies by shareholders or banks are subject to restriction. Bank loans may not exceed three times the amount of a company's registered capital. Borrowings from the public may not exceed ten times the registered capital.

Mutual Funds

There are two kinds of investment fund companies:

The first is the "open end" investment fund. An open-ended fund does not have a fixed capital. Its aim is to sell as many shares (or units) as it can to increase the size of the fund. Since the concept of a trust is unknown in Luxembourg, a separate management company is needed to run an open ended fund. The issued and fully paid capital of the management company must be at least $110,000.

The second is the "closed end" investment company. This starts with

219

a fixed amount of capital. Like any other company it can increase its issued share capital. The excess of the issue price over the par value of its shares can be used to finance the redemption of its shares. Redemption is provided through a repurchase holding company (completely owned by the investment company) which may re-sell shares to the public. There are certain regulations concerning the relationship between the investment and repurchase company, particularly concerning the proportion of premiums to par value, the information required in the published accounts of the companies concerned and other matters.

The "milliard" is simply a holding company with capital exceeding L.Fr. 1,000 million. It is granted special low tax rates. It may choose to be taxed either as a milliard company or as a standard holding company. Once it chooses, it cannot change its mind. If it is to be taxed as a milliard, the minimum tax is L.Fr. 1.6 million.

The following are the approximate costs of forming a holding company:

Share Capital	Registration Taxes 1.1.1973 1%	Inscription In Business Register, etc.	Memorial Publication (approx.)	Notary Fees (approx.)	Miscellaneous Inc. V.A.T.	Total Forma Costs e Profess Fees
$	$	$	$	$	$	$
3,000	30	45	175	50	40	34
20,000	200	65	175	80	45	56
100,000	1,000	85	175	250	75	1,58
500,000	5,000	100	175	760	150	6,18
1,000,000	10,000	100	175	1,010	190	11,47
5,000,000	50,000	100	175	2,180	320	52,77
20,000,000	200,000	100	175	3,540	500	204,31

Luxembourg law also recognizes the following forms of doing business:
1. the société en nom collectif (general partnership);
2. the société en commandite simple (limited partnership);
3. the société en commandite par actions (company limited by shares, but having one or more general partners);
4. the société à responsabilité limitée (limited liability company);
5. the société cooperative (cooperative company).

Tax
Holding Companies

A Luxembourg holding company that meets all the requirements for tax benefits will be free from corporation and profits tax, from tax on dividends and interest it receives, capital gains tax, wealth tax, withholding taxes on dividends paid to its shareholders, withholding taxes on bond interest payments, stamp duty on the securities it may issue and "winding up" taxes.

All Luxembourg companies, including the holding company, are subject to an annual subscription tax on the amount of their issued share capital. Standard S.A. companies are taxed at a rate of 0.36% and holding companies at 0.16%. The minimum annual subscription tax is L.Fr. 1,500. In addition a registration tax of 1% is payable on the issue of securities and on an increase in share capital. The minimum annual registration tax is L.Fr. 3,000.

Milliard holding companies are exempted from annual subscription tax and pay registration tax at reduced rates. Milliard companies are taxable, however, from 0.1% to 3% on interest paid on bonds, dividend distributions and salaries or fees paid to foreign managers and directors residing outside Luxembourg for more than six months of the year. The minimum annual milliard company tax is L.Fr. 1.6 million.

One disadvantage of Luxembourg, compared with several other noted tax havens, is that all the double tax agreements to which Luxembourg is a party specifically *exclude* holding companies from the benefits of any reductions in the rates of withholding tax on dividends, interest or royalties received from the other partner country. This has induced companies to consider incorporating in other tax sheltered areas.

Companies

Ordinary Luxembourg S.A. companies are subject to tax on their world-wide income. Deductions allowed from gross income include standard business expenses and 50% of any income from a foreign permanent establishment if that income was taxed at its foreign source. Companies are considered resident if they are incorporated or founded under Luxembourg law or if their principal place of management is in Luxembourg.

Non-resident companies are taxed on profits from a Luxembourg establishment.

The standard corporate income tax rate is 40%. Companies with income below L.Fr. 1,312,000 are charged lower rates.

Dividends are subject to a 15% withholding tax when paid to residents. Dividends paid to non-residents from ordinary companies may be taxed at reduced rates because of double tax treaties.

Dividends received by a Luxembourg company from another resident company in which it directly owns at least 25% of the voting power and has held this ownership for a minimum of 12 months are exempt from corporation and withholding tax. Where the dividend is received from a

221

non-resident company, a 50% exemption is allowed if the foreign company is subject to corporate taxes similar to those of Luxembourg. This 50% exemption is also granted if: a) two or more resident companies own a minimum of 25% of a non-resident company, and b) one of the recipient companies owns over 50% of the capital of the other recipient company.

Losses can be carried forward for five years, but no carry-back is permitted.

Individuals

Personal income tax rates are progressive with the peak rate set at 57%. A resident for tax purposes is one who maintains a home in Luxembourg or has his normal place of residence in the country. Non-residents are only taxed on income arising in Luxembourg. Taxable income is sub-divided into eight types and each category is allowed certain expense deductions. A number of expenses are deductible, including interest paid on business loans, depreciation, insurance premiums on property and land taxes. There is a minimum deduction of L.Fr. 12,000 for employment expenses though the taxpayer may prove and deduct a higher amount.

There is also a local trade tax on net trading profits over L.Fr. 200,000 of about 10%. This tax is a deductible expense.

A wealth tax is assessed annually at a 0.5% rate on the total net worth of assets of resident individuals and companies. Non-residents pay this tax only in respect of certain specified assets located in Luxembourg. (This minimum net wealth tax is L.Fr. 2,500 for resident companies.) Residents are permitted an exemption of L.Fr. 100,000 if single, and 200,000 if married and 100,000 for each dependent child. There is also a local business asset tax of about 0.5%. The individual exemption for this tax is L.Fr. 500,000 of assets.

Value-Added Tax

The general rate of value-added tax is 10% with a reduced rate of 5% for certain specific goods and services, and a temporary 2% rate for some foods and pharmaceutical products.

Stock Exchange

The Luxembourg stock market is one of the more active European exchanges although it has a low turnover. It has over 1,000 listings and is heavily involved in Eurobond issues. Many foreign companies find Luxembourg an easy place to get a listing and the status that comes with it is advantageous.

222   The Luxembourg Bourse is under the control of the Bank Commission.

Employment

Any foreigner (except EEC nationals) wanting to work in Luxembourg needs a permit from the Office National du Travail in Luxembourg. Application for the permit is made by the prospective employer.

The directors of a firm applying for a trading license are required to produce the following documents:

1. Extrait du Casier Judiciaire—This is a police record which is issued by the Court of Justice for residents. Applicants should submit an affidavit that their firm has never been adjudged bankrupt.

2. Certificate d'Aptitude Professionelle (CAP)—This is a certificate proving professional and technical competence. It certifies that the individual concerned has been employed in the trade he has decided to invest in for a minimum of three years.